RUNNING SHORTS

STAN GREENBERG

Illustrations by David Arthur

GUINNESS PUBLISHING

ACKNOWLEDGEMENTS

Alastair Aitken, Pat Brian, Mark Butler, Roger Gynn, Matti Hannus (*Finland*), Ian Hodge, Richard Hymans, Peter Lovesey, Peter Matthews, Norris McWhirter, Roberto Quercetani (*Italy*), Colin Shields, Bob Sparks, Mel Watman, Alf Wilkins, The Guinness Book of Records, IAAF publications, Track & Field News, Athletics Today, Athletics Weekly, Athletics World, British and foreign newspapers, Members of the NUTS and ATFS, and their publications

Published in Great Britain by Guinness Publishing Ltd, 33 London Road, Enfield, Middlesex

Cover illustration by Paul Finn

Designed by Kathleen Aldridge

Typeset in Palatino by Ace Filmsetting Ltd, Frome, Somerset

Printed and bound in Great Britain by The Bath Press, Bath

"Guinness" is a registered trademark of Guinness Publishing Ltd

A catalogue record for this book is available from the British Library

ISBN 0–85112–507–7

ABOUT THE AUTHOR

Stan Greenberg knows exactly the day which changed his life –
31 July 1948. Until then he had been a dedicated fan of both
Spurs and Arsenal, a strange circumstance perhaps explained
by the fact that the two teams had shared White Hart Lane
during the war. But that day was his first experience of
watching athletics, and an Olympic Games, and he was
completely overwhelmed by the colour and excitement. He
never again attended a soccer match, immersing himself in
athletics statistics and history. As a participant, he had been a
fairly good club sprinter, but rarely trained hard enough. He
played football at work, making the first team, more because of
his speed on the wing than for his woeful ball-control. While a
consistent scorer, he nevertheless missed the goal far more
often, mainly, according to his teammates, due to his habit of
'toe-punting'. However, he still claims that he often put it in the
net, direct from corner-kicks, with his patented sliced toe-punt.
As a badminton player he reached the finals of the London
Business Houses championships, and still regards the game
with fondness.

For many years merely a hobby, his athletics interests led to
him assisting the BBC TV commentators as a statistician, and he
has done this for 25 years, at every major athletics occasion.
Barcelona was his eighth Olympic Games. Having previously
worked in industry and local government, he spent six happy
years as sports editor of *The Guinness Book of Records*. In 1982, he
became a freelance, still primarily working for the BBC athletics
team, but also producing books, including a well-received one
on the Olympic Games published by Guinness.

CONTENTS

ON YOUR MARKS

HEART-FELT The winner of the 1920 English National Cross-Country championships was the great French runner Joseph Guillemot, who later in the year won the Olympic 5000m title. A doctor had been given permission to conduct some tests, and checked the leading runners with his stethoscope. He had quite a shock when he checked Guillemot as the Frenchman had no heartbeat – and presumably was therefore dead. It took a little while before the shaken medic could be informed that Guillemot's heart was actually on his *right* side. Incidentally, the Frenchman had survived and overcome the effects of a gas attack during the First World War.

UNITED NATIONS With just a few laps to go in the 1964 Olympic 10 000 metres final, Ron Clarke of Australia looked behind at his three closest rivals, the only ones capable of mounting a challenge. Clarke had already done enough in his running career to put him in the Pantheon of the world's greatest, but he dearly wanted to crown his achievements with an Olympic gold medal. Ever since, as a 19-year-old junior record holder, he had been given the honour of bringing the torch into the stadium in Melbourne at the 1956 Games, he had dreamed of such a moment. At Tokyo he felt that moment had come.

The best and most famous runners in the world had been broken by the pace of Clarke's early running and now, as he looked over his shoulder, all he saw were three virtual unknowns: an Ethiopian, a North African Arab and an American Indian. He probably didn't realise at the time just what a microcosm of sport that

was – the Tokyo Games had witnessed a record 93 countries entering competitors, a record which would increase by over 80 per cent by 1992. On the last lap only the member of the Ethiopian Emperor's bodyguard was dropped, and Clarke had to give way eventually to both the Tunisian Gammoudi and the winner, American Marine Billy Mills.

STARTING AND FINISHING Colonel Evan Hunter, onetime Secretary of the British Olympic Association, was one of the best known starters in Britain. At his memorial service a passage from Psalm 121 proved marvellously apt: 'He will not suffer thy foot to be moved.'

WHICH ONE? There is a story, no doubt apocryphal, about an athletics team visiting Wales which went for a short sight-seeing tour into the valleys. When it was time to go, it was realised that their sprinter Jones was missing, so the team manager climbed up on a mound and bawled out 'J–O–N–E–S'. After a few minutes back came the echo, 'Which Jones?'

COMMENTATOR'S NIGHTMARES In one of the heats of the 1972 Olympic 100m, commentators were shocked to note that two of the competitors were Vassilios Papageorgopoulos of Greece and Jean-Louis Ravelomanantsoa of Madagascar.

They were able to take some comfort that another two sprinters, Benedict Majekodunmi of Nigeria and Sunil Gunawardene of Sri Lanka, had been put in a different heat.

Madagascar can claim to have some of the most difficult names in the world. Sadistic fans are hoping that their 400m runner, Randriamahazomanana, makes it to the next Olympics – and we don't even know his first name. Mind you, even if he isn't there, perhaps his decathlete teammate will be – and his name is Elie Razafindrakovahoaka. In similar vein, some older fans fondly remember the Singhalese high-jumper Nagalingham Ethirveerasingham.

At the 1991 World championships faint hearts missed a beat on noting the Mongolian distance entry, who rejoiced in the name Tschuuluunbaatar Ariunsaikhan. Fortunately for some, he did not get past the heats of the 5000m or 10 000m.

The other side of the coin is not necessarily much better. There are invariably problems with the pronunciation of short names, and a recent example was the Japanese women's 10km runner, Oe. She can claim to be the one with the shortest name who runs the longest distance in a world-class time, her best being 33:17.97 in 1991. Back at the 1936 Olympics her namesake Sueo Oe became the shortest-named athletics medallist ever when he took the bronze in the pole vault.

A slightly different problem arises with some names. One of the best recent examples was the Korean sprinter at the 1988 Olympic Games with the mind-boggling name (in English anyway) of Shim Duk-Sup. Any fan of the Marx Brothers will have trouble with that one.

One other nightmare for a commentator is the similarity of certain names. One can imagine the problems caused by different athletes named Smith, Jones or Davis, but a greater potential for confusion was caused by the emergence in the 1980s of two world-class American 400m runners named Walter McCoy and Antonio McKay. However, perhaps the greatest test of a commentator's nerve occurred in the 1992 African championships 400m hurdles final for women. The field included Nigerian twins Omatoyo and Omolade Akinremi as well as their older sister Taiya. Later they ran the first three legs of the winning 4 × 400m relay team.

BUT OF COURSE Some years ago at a murder trial in Belfast the accused was found to be insane. In supporting the medical evidence for the man's condition, counsel stated that his only interest in life was athletics.

IF YOU'RE A LOSER, YOU'RE A LOSER In a Chicago street in the late 1960s a man was moving surreptitiously from car to car, testing to see if the doors could be forced. As he concentrated on a particular car he suddenly heard a shout and saw, some distance away, a middle-aged black man come rushing out of a building towards him. Not too disturbed, he began to run away but realised that the irate car owner was gaining. Despite giving it all he had, the thief was soon overtaken and held until the police arrived. When he was informed who his intended victim was, he shook his head and muttered, 'I've always been a loser. Only me would try and rob Jesse Owens.'

Jesse gives chase – thief gives up!

A similar story was reported in South Africa in 1992. Elana Meyer, who had set national records over 3000m, 5000m, 10 000m and 15km, was out training when a lady's bag got snatched by a thief quite nearby. She gave chase and although the criminal got away by vaulting over a wall, she was able to retrieve the bag for the thankful owner.

AS THE SAYING GOES Kenyan cross-country teams have shown incredible strength in the World Championships in recent years, with their scoring runners getting to the front of races and holding virtually unbeatable positions. Those trying to understand this remarkable example of team running may have gained some insight from a recent article in a magazine. The writer, Bob Hancock, once taught in a Kenyan school and he notes that there is a saying in Swahili, 'Umoja ni nguvu', which means 'Unity is strength'. He suggests that the notion that the strength of the team is greater than the sum of the strengths of its individual members has been well and truly proven.

TRAINING AIDS Athletes are always on the lookout for new or improved aids to training and competition. Even if only in the mind, a new wrinkle may provide the small improvement which can make the difference from being an also-ran to becoming the champion. Thus much interest was shown in a recent discussion about the benefits or otherwise of sexual relations prior to a competition. Traditionally, especially in boxing, sportsmen and women have been told to abstain for a period before the big event. In the 1980s there were ripples caused when a Colorado State University study indicated that sporting results showed no difference when the athletes tested had or had not.

Recently the famous sex therapist, Dr Ruth Westheimer, has stated that if one is looking at the quick emotional release, it could be very beneficial, although she considered that 'a whole-night affair' would not be. She further noted that if an athlete thinks that doing or not doing something will help them win, and that belief is a strong one, then it will probably work. So there you are.

PUNS A recent meeting in Seville, Spain, gave rise to a number of athletic puns – which are no better nor worse than any others of the genre. The back-up timing officials were referred to, understandably, as 'Manuel' timers; it was suggested that the Algerian winner of the 1500m should be known as the 'Berber of Seville'; while the Spanish distance runner Martin Fiz was deemed to have 'sparkle'.

A less clever, perhaps insulting comment was made during the 1936 Olympic pole vault final in which the Japanese vaulters gave the Americans unexpected opposition, leading to the obvious remark that there was 'a nip in the air'.

THE FIRST ATHLETICS PROMOTER? In *Charles Dickens: His Tragedy and Triumph*, Vol. 2 pp 1056–1057, there is a reference to the great writer promoting a 'day of foot races' for working men in a meadow near his home at Chatham, Kent, sometime about 1865. This is one of the earliest references to a 'promoter'.

WHAT VEST? The rule relating to athletes wearing their club colours took on a whole new meaning at a meeting held in Gainesville, USA, in April 1991. It was reported that about 45 men and women from ten college teams took part in the Nude Relays, secretly racing nude on the University of Florida track. One must hope that the winner's medals were warmed before presentation.

CROSS-COUNTRY The longest cross-country run in the world is thought to be the 30km (*18.6 miles*) Lidingoloppet held annually near Stockholm, Sweden. The largest ever field was in 1982 when there were 11 763 starters. It has been suggested that some inmates of a certain institution on the Isle of Wight have run further until caught by officers from the establishment (Parkhurst Prison).

While not wishing to propagate the myth of Irish feyness, I am reminded of the notice put up in the Press room at the 1979 IAAF Cross-Country championships at Limerick which stated, 'It will be dry all day – except for intermittent rain.'

Later in the day the announcer asked the crowd, 'Is there anybody here who can open a locked door without a key?' Apparently, some equipment was needed from a locked storage cupboard.

THE COLD WAR At the height of the Cold War, the Soviet Union participated in the Olympic Games for the first time when they appeared in strength at Helsinki in 1952. They were much criticised for housing their competitors in a separate village, well away from the other teams, but the IOC did not protest too much as everyone was pleased that they had turned up at all. In fact, it should be said that individual Soviet athletes seemed to be quite friendly with their opposite numbers from elsewhere. However, a particular situation occurred in the steeplechase which was tailor-made for the Western press. The event was won, for the first time since 1904, by an American who beat the Soviet favourite. The fact that caused such jocularity was that the winner, Horace Ashenfelter, was an FBI agent. The headline 'FBI agent followed by Soviet' was too good not to be used.

There is a story, which I am assured is true, that comes from Britain's first match against the Soviet Union in Moscow. Prior to departure the team were given strict instructions about loose talk, especially the few service personnel who had been selected, and warned that their rooms would probably be bugged. On arrival, two of the servicemen were put into a rather spartan room on the first floor of the hotel. They immediately searched for any such listening devices, but failed to find anything until one of them noticed that the only rug on the floor was under a strangely placed small table in the middle of the room. Closer examination revealed a highly suspicious screw-like object in the floor, under the rug. With a look of triumph in their eyes they started to unscrew the object . . . and

A crash course in room security

down in the foyer the chandelier crashed to the floor.

There is an unbelievable pettiness exhibited by some of the media when politics intrudes into sport. One of the worst examples

happened during the 1980 Olympic Games in Moscow. Much of the West supported President Carter's boycott of these Games, ostensibly because of the Soviet Union's shameful invasion of Afghanistan – though it was noticeable that trade with the pariah was hardly affected. Certain sections of the British press, not the sportswriters let it be said, had obviously been instructed to 'knock' as much as possible. Thus one had the ludicrous report of Soviet officials opening a door at one end of the vast Lenin Stadium every time one of their javelin competitors threw. A greater effect would have been had by asking the crowd to blow. Perhaps even worse, to an athletics fan, was the report that the door was at the end behind the throwers. Apparently the authors of the report were unaware that an assisting wind for a javelin in those days needed to come from the front.

SING IT AGAIN, SAM Not for the first time athletics beat soccer to it. Luciano Pavarotti's singing at the opening of the 1990 World Cup soccer competition had been anteceded by another great tenor, Jussi Bjorling, who had sung at the opening ceremony of the 1958 European athletics championships in Stockholm.

IS THAT YOU? There have been statues erected to a number of champion athletes. Perhaps the most famous is that of Paavo Nurmi outside the Olympic stadium in Helsinki, Finland. Others include that of Fanny Blankers-Koen outside the Zoological Gardens in Rotterdam, Holland; Grete Waitz outside the Bislett Stadium in Oslo, Norway; and Arthur Wint in Kingston, Jamaica. In fact the latter is only partly of Wint, as it is apparently an amalgam of the Jamaican 4 × 400m relay team which won the 1952 Olympic gold medal: Wint, Herb McKenley, Les Laing and George Rhoden.

THAT WILL DO NICELY When the Olympic Games were held in Los Angeles in 1932, the Coliseum track was the only one in the United States which was exactly 400 metres in circumference – all the many others were 440 yards.

TEA FOR TWO Some people are fascinated by twins in sport. One of the best performances by them must be when the medley relay team of Wayne and Blaine Rideout and Elmer and Delmer Brown, representing North Texas State college, broke the indoor 'world record' for the event at the Millrose Games in 1938. The Rideouts were among the top milers of their time and were of remarkably similar ability. In 1938 they both ran 9:04.4 for 2 miles indoors. Then the following year, within six weeks, Blaine ran a mile in 4:10.9 outdoors and Wayne ran the same time indoors.

Though not of the same high standard, Robert and Ross Hume of Michigan University tied for the 1944 NCAA mile title in 4:16.6. In recent years the Argentinian walking twins Benjamin and Jorge Lorefice tied for the national 20km walk record (1hr28:19) in 1990 and the 50km walk mark (4hr17:03) in 1991. In 1992 they tied for the national 20km title.

AND THEN THERE WERE THREE The only known case of triplets representing their country at athletics is that of the Svoboda family of Czechoslovakia. In 1927 Alois (high jump), Jiri (javelin) and Joseph (discus) were all selected for the national team.

FAST, FASTER, GULP In an appendix to a learned paper on 'Velocity of Mammal Movement' some years ago, there was an entry under 'Species – Man' which noted that a Masai warrior had been timed at 18.4mph (*29.6 km/h*) when being chased by a rhinoceros. A rather more sinister listing further down under 'Species – African Rhinoceros', quoting the same source, noted that a rhinoceros had been clocked at 27.2mph (*43.7 km/h*) 'when chasing a Masai warrior'. Ouch!

THE HARD WAY When John Savidan of New Zealand won the Empire Games 6 mile title in 1930 (his country's first ever gold medal in a major championship), he had really given his all. There was very little of Savidan to start with, only 126lbs (*57 kg*), but he had what is now called 'the right stuff'. For one thing, it was to be his racing debut at the distance – he was primarily selected for the 3 miles – and staggeringly he had run a 6 mile time trial a few days before the Games in 100 degree heat. Second, he insisted on marching with the rest of the New Zealand team in the opening ceremony parade, just hours before the start of his race.

Then to the race itself, in which he found that the English and Scottish runners were slowing and speeding up the pace in efforts to destroy each other. Finally he took the lead himself just after halfway. Forcing the pace, he opened up a healthy lead but was very pleased to see the lap board indicate only one lap to go. With the crowd applauding him he increased his pace, wanting to give it everything, and drove off the final bend towards the tape. Except there was no tape – which surprised him but he thought it was just difficult for the officials with so many lapped runners. He crossed the line, only to hear the officials shouting 'another lap'. He also heard the gun fire (in Canada they used that American custom to indicate the last lap instead of the European one of ringing a bell).

Seeing the Englishman Ernie Harper – who had been nearly half a lap behind him – coming down the straight, Savidan set off again, struggling badly. Harper, who had been taking it fairly easy, assured of second place, now realised that something was wrong with the stumbling figure ahead and set off after him. The crowd was going wild, urging Savidan onward. Somehow the little New Zealander kept going and finally fell through the tape still over 50 yards ahead. He had won. He decided to miss the 3 miles later in the week, but nobody from New Zealand minded one bit.

WHAT'S IN A NAME The habit of statisticians hyphenating the new names of female athletes who get married, with their maiden names, reached an all-time high (or low) in the case of a British international of the 1920s. Her maiden name was Sophia Peirce-Evans; she then married a Mr Elliott-Lynn, then remarried and became Lady Heath. Thus in lists – causing untold space problems – she becomes Sophia Peirce-Evans-Elliott-Lynn-Heath.

The mispronunciation of names is an acrimonious topic in athletic circles and our Transatlantic cousins are firmly to the fore in this area. One of their top distance runners, Doug Padilla, was running at Crystal Palace on one occasion and was asked for the correct way to say his name. He said it was Pa-dill-a. The author protested that this couldn't be right – it was surely Pa-di-ya (i.e. the Spanish pronunciation). The American laughed and confirmed that this way was correct, of course, but he had given up with American commentators.

One of the competitors in the 1991 World Student Games marathon was Godknows Tefe from Ghana. Unfortunately he got cramp three times during the race and God knows he wanted to give up. But he didn't and finished last in 3hr17:37.

During the 1958 European championships in Stockholm, the British team's interpreter got into difficulties with the names of the middle distance runners, Rawson, Johnson and Hewson. Also running for Norway was Boysen.

There was a lively exchange at the 1968 Olympic Games when one of the American experts, Dick Bank (known to be a wealthy man), met British runner Lillian Board. Always a punster, Dick asked her, 'Are you the British Board?' To which Lillian snapped back, 'Are you the Bank of America?'

THE AGE-OLD QUESTION The announcement in 1991 that the official strip of the Stranraer and District Highland Games Club consists of 'white T-shirt and kilt' leaves the ancient mystery unanswered for non-Scots. Surely for running events their athletes

would also wear . . .! Mind you, they're a hardy lot north of the border.

THE NATIVES ARE RESTLESS
In 1972 the famous British runner Bruce Tulloh went to north-western Mexico to visit the Tarahumara Indians, who are renowned for their running abilities. While there he took the opportunity to run against some of them at distances up to 9 miles (14.5km). He discovered that they found such distances 'too short', as their great traditional runs lasted for 2–3 days covering distances of over 150 miles (240km). During these races they would often run 60 miles (97km) in 10 hours. He met one man, aged about 45, who had won one race of approximately 161 miles (259km) in about 36 hours. Two 12-year-old boys ran in an 8-hour race and some women took part in a 60-mile event. Their main sport is 'rarajipari' in which, while racing over long distances over rough terrain, a ball has to be kicked and kept in play all the way by three-man teams. It is not known if any of the current crop of excellent distance runners being produced by Mexico have any affiliation to this tribe.

DING-DONG BELL An entertaining moment for spectators at the 1978 Commonwealth Games came during the second semi-final of the 5000m. As the runners approached the start of the last lap, an over-zealous official rang the bell a little too vigorously and it literally fell apart. Happily, the incident had no effect on the runners, who included Henry Rono (the winner) and England's McLeod and Foster.

PASSPORT PLEASE There are a number of athletes whose names have geographic connotations which are not akin to the countries they have represented. The most notable of these have been the 1981 European Junior hurdles champion Holger Pohland who ran for East Germany; America's Michelle Finn who won the 1990 US 100m title; Britain's Rob Denmark who actually beat a Dane for the bronze medal at the 1991 World Indoor championships; John Holland of New Zealand who won the 1952 Olympic bronze medal in the 400m hurdles; and Maree Holland of Australia, a 1988 Olympic 400m finalist. Other recent examples include Eric Lichtenstajn who runs for Belgium; Courtenay Ireland, the New Zealand record holder in the shot; and Desmond English, an Irish 800m runner.

BARRIERS ARE FOR BREAKING The initial 'dream' performance was the 10-second 100 yards. The first amateur to achieve an acceptable even-time was Tom Bury at Cambridge in 1855. The first to officially 'break' the barrier was an American, John Owen, who ran 9⅘ths (i.e. 9.8) at Washington DC on 11 October 1890. The first woman to run under 11 seconds for 100m was Renate Stecher (GDR) in 1973.

The quest which gained most attention, however, was for the four-minute mile and as early as 1923 Paavo Nurmi, the great Finnish athlete, thought that he could get it. On one of the rare occasions that he attempted it he was 10.4 seconds out. The mythical barrier lasted until 6 May 1954 when Roger Bannister ran 3:59.4 at Oxford.

An intrinsically better achievement was the first sub-five minute clocking for 2000m, which went to Harald Norpoth of Germany with 4:57.8 in 1966. The first man to run under 3½ minutes for 1500m was Steve Cram (GBR) at Nice in 1985 (3:29.67), while the first sub-four minutes (for 1500m) by a woman was 3:56.0 by Tatyana Kazankina (URS) in 1976.

The first 6ft (*1.83m*) high jump came in 1876 when Marshall Brooks cleared that height at Oxford. Charlie Dumas (USA) was the first to 7ft (*2.13m*) when he went over 2.15m eighty years later. The 8ft (*8.44m*) jump was achieved by Javier Sotomayor (CUB) in 1989. The first 6ft clearance by a woman was by Iolanda Balas (ROM) in 1958.

The seemingly unattainable 20ft (*6.09m*) pole vault was made by Sergei Bubka (URS) with 6.10m in 1991. It should be noted that a 100m (*328ft 1in*) javelin throw was made, with the 'old' implement, when Uwe Hohn (GDR) reached 104.80m in 1984 – and thus caused the regulations to be changed in the interests of safety.

IT'S NOT OVER TILL THE FAT LADY SINGS It is an old adage in athletics that you must run 'through the tape', i.e. not ease up near the end of a race. However, there have been significant examples where those who should have known better have relaxed too early and lost. Probably the best known of these was the 5000m race at Crystal Palace in August 1980 when Olympic 800m champion Steve Ovett unwisely eased up in the last few strides and narrowly lost to a fast-finishing John Treacy of Ireland, the automatic times being 13:27.82 to 13:27.87.

Yet another case occurred at the 1991 World Championships in

Tokyo, in front of the eyes of millions (courtesy of television). In the heats of the 800m, with only two to qualify, one of the event's favourites, Tom McKean (GBR), eased disastrously, virtually on the line, and was eliminated by two fast-finishing athletes.

A good example to note in relation to the above situations was the statement by 1968 Olympic 400m champion and world-record holder Lee Evans. He once pointed out that the reason he was involved in so many close finishes was the fact that he was prepared to go 402 metres while his rivals quit after 398.

HARE-BRAINED The term 'hare', as used in athletics, comes from the old English pastime of hare and hounds running. This was where one or two athletes would set out on a cross-country run and would either set a paper trail or leave some other form of marker along the way so that the pursuing pack could follow their route – based very much on the way that foxes and hares were hunted from horses by the landed gentry. Indeed, many of the early clubs were named Harriers. Thus today, a person who makes the pace for a race is referred to as a hare. The misnomer, rabbit, used in some quarters, is incorrect and has come about in translation of the correct term into European languages.

The increased practice in recent years of having pace-makers in middle-distance races has regularly resulted in quite farcical situations. So often the designated hare has proceeded to do his job, at an agreed pace, only to find that the 'stars' are so busy watching each other that he is ignored and ends up running well ahead of the pack – a useless exercise for them

and for him. The classic case occurred at Oslo's Bislett stadium in June 1981 when the hare, Tom Byers (USA), was supposed to make a good pace for a top-class field. This included Steve Ovett, Steve Cram, John Walker, Steve Scott and Thomas Wessinghage, with the implication of a world record attempt.

Byers went off at a not particularly fast cadence, reaching 400m in 57.52 and 800m in 1:54.83. At this point the main body was some 50 metres behind and apparently not bothering. He kept going to reach the bell some 70 metres ahead and passed 1200m in 2:53.09. The pack now began to race each other and close the enormous gap on Byers who, though beginning to fade quite badly, had realised that he had a chance to win the race. Treading the proverbial 'water', he took 61.5 for his last lap, compared to Ovett's 52.3, but was able to hang on to the end and gain a famous victory. His final time was 3:39.01 with Ovett, the runner-up, a mere half-second behind. It is to the Briton's credit that he found the whole thing very funny. The promoter's reactions were not reported.

When Peter Snell (NZ) broke the world 880y/800m records on a grass track at Christchurch in February 1962, the report in a British national newspaper indicated the creative art of headline writers. In the race itself, the pace to halfway was made by Barry Robinson. As he slowed, Snell apparently had to move out to go around him before striking for home. No doubt the agency message mentioned this fact, which resulted in the headline, 'Snell breaks record despite nearly tripping over rabbit', and an imaginative story which implied that the great New Zealand runner had nearly fallen over a small furry creature.

Snell came haring off the bend . . .

A finalist in the 1991 US women's 3000m championships was Elisabeth 'Buffy' Rabbitt. Needless to say, sportswriters are eagerly awaiting the time when she is asked to make the pace in a race somewhere. Her brother receives even more smirks – his name is Roger.

OOPS! Though not recommended by most coaching manuals, there have been a number of spectacular falls from which athletes have recovered to win important races. The most famous one was the tumble taken by Lasse Viren (FIN) in the 1972 Olympic 10 000m final. Just before halfway in the race he suddenly tripped and fell,

bringing down the Tunisian Mohamed Gammoudi (the 1968 5000m champion). Although losing an estimated 5 seconds, the Finn was quickly up and back into his running and had caught the leaders by the end of the next lap. He went on to win the race and more remarkably, break the world record for the distance with 27:38.4.

In the 5000m final at the 1990 European championships in Split, Salvatore Antibo (ITA) 'did a Viren' right at the beginning of the race, running into Marcus O'Sullivan (IRE) and falling. He lost about 30 metres on the leader at that point but had plenty of time to recover and eventually won the title.

On a slightly different plane was the incident which happened in a heat of the 1928 Olympic steeplechase. The great Finnish runner Paavo Nurmi – already a legend in his lifetime – had decided to enter that event as well as the 10 000m (gold) and 5000m (silver). Unfamiliar with the event, he was having problems with the barriers and at one point fell into the water jump. A Frenchman, Lucien Duquesne, stopped and courteously helped the great man to his feet. Nurmi, who was known for his rather sour demeanour and lack of 'humanity', was obviously touched by this act of kindness in such an important race. He proceeded to shepherd the Frenchman for the remainder of the race, even inviting him to cross the line in first place. This the gallant French runner declined to do. In the final, despite running his fifth distance race in seven days, Nurmi gained the silver medal behind yet another Finn. The Frenchman finished in sixth place.

RELIGIOUS OBSERVANCE In the late 1950s a small Texas religious institution, Abilene Christian College (4500 students), not only produced the 1956 Olympic 100m and 200m champion, Bobby Joe Morrow, but also a $4 \times 110y$ relay team that set two world records.

The American team to the 1900 Olympic Games was primarily from a group of Eastern universities. On arrival in Paris it was found that a number of finals were to be held on Sunday and some of the universities instructed their athletes not to compete, while others left it up to the competitors' individual consciences. Thus a rather strange situation occurred.

Myer Prinstein had set a new world record of 7.50m (24ft 7¼in) prior to leaving the United States and led in the Saturday qualifying round with 7.17m. However, he was at Syracuse University, a strong Methodist institution which had refused permission for its students to compete on the Sunday, and therefore had to miss the final which was won by Alvin Kraenzlein of the University of Pennsylvania with a jump of 7.18m. Happily, the rules of the time allowed Prinstein's earlier jump to count and he did get the silver medal. The irony of it was that Prinstein was Jewish, whereas Kraenzlein was a Christian. Four years later, at St Louis, the ever-liberal Prinstein got his gold (he also won the triple jump), this time representing the Greater New York Irish AA.

FINLAY PETER DUNNE
(American author in 1898)

'IN MY YOUNGER DAYS IT WAS NOT CONSIDERED RESPECTABLE TO BE AN ATHLETE. AN ATHLETE WAS ALWAYS A MAN THAT WAS NOT STRONG ENOUGH TO WORK'

TO EACH HIS OWN Finland did not become an independent country until 1919. Prior to that it was a Grand Duchy of the Empire of Russia, and though allowed to enter a separate team in the Olympic Games, it was not allowed to have its own flag. Thus in 1912, although the Russian team won no gold medals, the Imperial flag was raised for the nine Finnish victories. This was particularly galling to Hannes Kolehmainen, the first of the 'Flying Finns', who won the 5km and 10km titles at Stockholm. He reportedly said he almost wished he had not won rather than watch the hated flag raised for his victories. It may have played a big part in persuading him to return in 1920 and win the marathon title – and have the pleasure of watching the Finnish standard raised.

LADIES FIRST Germany has always been one of the most powerful athletic nations in the world and never more so than in recent times when it was split into two separate entities. Surprisingly, it had to wait until the 1928 Games to win its first Olympic gold medal, and then it was a woman who did it: at Amsterdam Lina Radke won the 800m in world record time. Due to the state of exhaustion shown by some of the competitors the race was not on the programme again for 32 years.

HORSES FOR COURSES At least two champion horses have been named after athletes. The 1909 Derby and 2000 Guineas winner *Minoru*, owned by King Edward VII, was specifically named after a legendary Japanese sprinter, Minoru Fujii. In November 1902 Fujii was reputed to have been timed electrically at 10.24 for 100m at the Imperial University, Tokyo; the official world record at the time was 10.8.

The other horse was ridden by the winner of the 1936 Olympic Three-Day Event, and was named *Nurmi* after the Finnish distance-running multiple medallist of the 1920s, Paavo Nurmi.

NEVER SATISFIED After the Grand Prix meeting in Brussels in 1991 two of the American athletes were interviewed by the press about their performances. Sprinter Andre Cason said that 'technically, I did everything wrong'. High hurdler Tony Dees said that 'it was just one of those off days'. One wouldn't have known that they had both won their events, Cason beating Christie and Mitchell in 10.08 and Dees beating Renaldo Nehemiah, clocking 13.28.

> **ALDOUS HUXLEY** (author)
>
> *'LIKE EVERY OTHER INSTRUMENT MAN HAS INVENTED, SPORT CAN BE USED FOR GOOD AND EVIL PURPOSES. USED BADLY, IT CAN ENCOURAGE PERSONAL VANITY AND GROUP VANITY, GREEDY DESIRE FOR VICTORY AND EVEN HATRED FOR RIVALS, AND INTOLERANT ESPRIT DE CORPS AND CONTEMPT FOR PEOPLE WHO ARE BEYOND AN ARBITRARILY-SELECTED PALE'*

SLOW, SLOWER, SLOWEST At the 1991 World Student Games a competitor from Rwanda, Emmanuele Senzira, was lapped three times in his 5000m heat as he finished some 5½ minutes behind the winner.

Even more outstanding (I use the word advisedly) was Olmeus Charles of Haiti, who literally held up the 1976 Olympic Games by his tardiness. He had apparently been selected not on ability but because he was a friend of the then dictator of his country. In his heat of the 10 000m he was nearly 14 minutes behind the winner, and what is worse, over 8½ minutes behind the next to last man, clocking 42:00.11 – the slowest time ever recorded in Olympic history. A countryman, Dieudone Lamothe, finished his 5000m heat 5 minutes behind the next to last man, while Haiti's 1500m (men) representative was slower than all bar one of the 36 runners in the women's equivalent.

NEVER GIVE UP In 1928 Ilmari Salminen won the Finnish Olympic trial race over 5000m, but as his win was considered a fluke he was not selected for the Games. Four years later, at the same distance, he only came fourth and so missed out yet again. However, in 1936, as a 33-year-old Army sergeant with four children, he made the team for Berlin and won the gold medal in the historic 10000m when Finland gained all three medals. The finish was also the closest ever with Salminen only 0.2 seconds ahead of Arvo Askola. Five days later in the 5000m he tripped and fell with only 2 laps to go and ended up in fifth place.

Up until the American high hurdles trials in 1948, world record holder Harrison Dillard had not lost a race for two years, but in the final he hit a hurdle and fell. Under the strict code of selection he was out of the Olympic hurdles race but managed to qualify for the flat 100 metres. In London he won that, beating a top-class field, and added another gold medal in the relay. From an American point of view his absence didn't matter as they took all three medals in the hurdles anyway. Four years later he won his 'own' event at the Helsinki Games and added another relay gold to his tally.

ANIMAL ANTICS In Peter Lovesey's *Official Centenary History of the AAA*, he records that in the 1868 championships, held at the Beaufort House track, the winner of the 440y title, Edward Colbeck,

beat the existing world mark despite a most bizarre encounter on the last bend. He collided with a sheep – the ground was shared with a farmer. Nevertheless Colbeck clocked 50.4, which was not bettered for 11 years. The sheep apparently suffered a broken leg.

During the early 1950s the White City, London, hosted the Caledonian Games, a Scottish festival of dancing, sheep trials and sport. At the 1951 version the British record holder Alan Paterson was just about to attempt the winning height in the high jump when one of the sheep broke away from the centre area and ran straight under the bar. As a Scot himself it may be that he had suffered such interruptions before, and undeterred, he jumped clear.

WHAT, NO FLOWERS? Author and coach Tom McNab claims to be the only man in Britain to have bought his wife a hammer (a 16lb ball attached to a length of chain) for her birthday, in 1991. He was vindicated when she won the event at the World Vets Championships later that year.

LIGHTNING DOES STRIKE TWICE At the 1991 World championships, held in Tokyo, Hassiba Boulmerka became the first Algerian woman to win a world title in any sport when she took the 1500m crown. The following day her countryman Noureddine Morceli, undeniably the favourite, won the men's 1500m gold medal. It was the first time at such a level that the winners of both the men's and women's 1500m had been from the same country.

'Is this your idea of a joke?'

At the Tokyo Olympic Games of 1964, Mary Rand won the long jump to become the first British woman athlete to win an Olympic gold medal. Four days later her team-mate Lynn Davies surprisingly won the men's long jump crown, the first time a Briton had won that title.

ROADHOGS In the heats of the 1984 Olympic 400m, Innocent Egbunike of Nigeria was drawn in the inside lane. With fairly easy qualifying conditions (first three) and no opposition of great note, he must have felt quietly confident. However, soon after the gun had fired he found that the athlete in lane two, Secundino Borabota of Equatorial Guinea – who quite probably had never run in lanes before – had cut into his lane and was blocking his way. For 100 metres or more the Nigerian ran behind the offender, screaming at him to get out of his lane. The bulk of the field were now well on their way. Eventually Egbunike was able to squeeze past Borabota, and making up a lot of ground over the last half of the race, he won in, not surprisingly, the slowest time of the day. The bewildered Borabota was disqualified.

Three athletes from Mozambique who were in Sheffield, England for the 1991 World Student Games, found a nice stretch of fairly straight road on which to train, not far from the Don Valley Stadium. Unfortunately they were apprehended by the police and charged with running on the M1.

UP, AND AT 'EM One of the most significant factors affecting athletic performance is altitude. Originally

'Take the next exit, please, gentlemen'

it was only considered to help certain `explosive' events when held at an altitude of 1000m or more, but now it is realised that much lower heights can still assist performance in sprints and jumps. However, in recent years it has become very obvious that there is another aspect to this assistance, and that is related to people born and/or living and training at excess altitude. A considerable part of the successes of athletes from Kenya, Ethiopia, Morocco and Mexico can be apportioned to the fact that many of their athletes come from high-altitude centres.

Probably the first time that notice was taken of the phenomenon was when the Pan-American Games were held at Mexico City (2240m/ 7347ft) in 1955. At this meeting Lou Jones (USA) smashed the world 400m record with 45.4, with Jim Lea (USA) also under the old mark with 45.6. However, it was only when American athletes started training and competing at Echo Summit, California in preparation for the Olympic Games in Mexico City in 1968 that the full effects of altitude assistance were realised. The Games themselves more than confirmed that hypothesis, and also confirmed the adverse effect on middle and distance races.

The greatest altitude at which a major championships has been held is 3630m (11 906ft) at La Paz, Bolivia for the 1981 South American title meet. The highest known track in the world is at Lhasa, Tibet, at an altitude of 4570m (14 990ft). The highest track in Europe is at Sestriere, Italy, which is at 2050m (6724ft). The highest in Britain is the 155m (508ft) altitude of the Gateshead stadium.

The famous track at Zurich, Switzerland is at a mere 410m (1345ft), but there is evidence to suggest that even at such a 'low' altitude sprinters, particularly, derive some benefit. Nevertheless, international statisticians have established the cut-off point of 1000m above sea level, above which performances are notated with an 'A' indicating altitude assistance.

EYE SAY, EYE SAY For many years Edward Smouha justly had a grievance against Olympic historians. Practically all books that listed the full names of medal-winning relay teams showed his brother Ellis as a member of the British sprint relay team which placed third at Amsterdam in 1928. Living abroad for the greater part of his post-athletics life, he had little opportunity to rectify the error until the early 1980s. At Cambridge University he was particularly remembered for his eccentricity of wearing his monocle while he sprinted.

LOOK HERE UPON THIS PICTURE (*Hamlet*) In recent years there have been numerous representations of athletes on stamps of various countries, but the first such was included in the set issued in Greece for the first modern Olympic Games in 1896, and depicts the famous statue, Discobolus, by Myron. For the 1928 Games the Netherlands produced an issue which included stylised pictures of a runner and a shot putter. However, it was not until 1932, in an American set issued to finance the Los Angeles Games, that an actual athlete was shown, on the 3 cent stamp. The model was a sprinter, J Alfred LeConey, who had won a gold medal in the 1924 sprint relay, but his features were unrecognisable as American law does not allow living persons to be featured on stamps.

Three years later, in 1935, Colombia commemorated their National Games with stamps which included the first recognisable athletes, in a representation of the finish of the 1912 Olympic 5000m between Hannes Kolehmainen (FIN) and Jean Bouin (FRA). South America also produced the first stamp depicting a female athlete, in an Ecuadorean issue of 1939 showing national sprinter Carola Castro winning the previous year's Bolivar Games title.

The first British athlete to be featured on a stamp was Lord Burghley, the 1928 400m hurdles champion, in a 1957 Dominican Republic set of Olympic gold medallists. The same year another issue included Chris Brasher, winner of the 1956 steeplechase, and the British-born New Zealander Norman Read who had won the 50km walk at Melbourne. However, in a 1950 Belgian set for the 4th European Athletic Championships, one stamp shows two unknown British relay runners changing the baton.

The first British sports stamps issue – a set of four with symbolic designs only – was for the 1948 Olympic Games in London. A three-stamp set issued by Britain in 1958 on the occasion of the VIth British Empire and Commonwealth Games in Cardiff were the first to commemorate that series of Games.

GET SET

BABY, IT'S COLD OUTSIDE

Indoor athletics has developed because of the need of European and east coast American athletes, particularly in the sprints and jumps, to continue their training and competition during the cold, wet and snowy winter months. The need was not so great for middle and distance runners, although nowadays they take advantage of such facilities as well.

The first known organised indoor athletics meeting was held in 1863 at the Ashburnham Hall, London, and consisted of five events. Five years later the New York Athletic Club organised a meeting which was the forerunner of the highly successful indoor meets held in the USA until recent times. That meeting was held in a building which later became the Empire City Skating Rink. Britain was the first European country to hold national indoor championships, in 1935 on a track laid, coincidentally, at the Empire Pool, Wembley. The United States had inaugurated their championships in 1906 at Madison Square Garden, New York, after an unofficial gathering 18 years earlier.

The early tracks were limited in size by the buildings they were housed in and tended in the main to be from 140–160y in circumference. Later, and particularly in Europe, there was great variation in size. The track laid in the enormous Houston Astrodome in 1968 measured 322m, while some 'fieldhouses' and 'armouries' in the USA and Finland are large enough to stage indoor hammer and javelin competitions. It was only when purpose-built stadia were constructed in the 1960s that some standardisation was attempted, with 200m the popular norm.

IN THE BEGINNING

There is no doubt that once mankind consolidated its foothold on the earth and progressed beyond day-to-day existence and survival, athletic contests to decide the fleetest, or the furthest spear-thrower, must certainly have occurred. Such contests must have been the first 'sporting' endeavours attempted by our forebears. In his book *Championship Technique in Track and Field*, published in 1941, the famous American coach Dean Cromwell describes what at first seems to be a sprint race but turns out to be a run by a mythical prehistoric man (Steve Stoner) to get away from a sabre-toothed tiger.

The Tailteann Games in Ireland are thought to date from *c.* 1829 BC, while the precursors to the ancient Olympic Games in Greece are thought to have been celebrated *c.* 1300 BC. Historical evidence dates the Olympic Games themselves to 900 BC, and the first firm records date from 776 BC, when the first known champion was Coroibis in the stade (approximately 192m) foot race. Throughout the Middle Ages in Europe there are reports of athletic feats of one sort or another, and we know that among the Indians in North and South America distance running was practised to a marked degree, albeit usually as part of religious ritual. There are also references in the Old Testament to those with athletic abilities, although there is no indication that they were of a competitive kind.

As far as modern athletics is concerned, the first school to hold inter-class sports was Eton, in England, in 1837. The earliest-known report of an organised athletics meeting was one held by the University of Oxford on 4 December 1860, which led to the first match against Cambridge University on 5 March 1864. The first recorded inter-club match was between Birchfield and Liverpool Harriers at Liverpool on 12 May 1883; it was won by the home club.

ROOM AT THE TOP Possibly the most successful room at an Olympic Games was that shared by four British girls in Tokyo in 1964. The occupants of that room were Mary Rand, Ann Packer, Mary Peters and Pat Pryce. Rand won the long jump with a world record-breaking performance, gained silver in the pentathlon and a bronze in the 4 × 100m relay; Packer won the 800m in world record time and gained silver in the 400m in her third improvement to the British mark; Peters placed fourth in the pentathlon; and Pryce broke the British record in the 80m hurdles, only just failing to make the final. Some of the magic of that room must have hung around as Peters went on to win the 1972 pentathlon with a new world record.

In Barcelona in 1992 Quincy Watts and Kevin Young shared a room in the American quarters. Watts won the 400m with the second fastest time ever and was part of the world record-breaking 4 × 400m relay team. Young not only won the 400m hurdles but in doing so set a fabulous new record of 46.78.

TRUTH IS STRANGER THAN FICTION When the 1948 Olympic team was announced, someone wrote that 'Mal Whitfield (800m) will run till he wins, Curtis Stone (5000m) will run till he drops, and

Henry Laskau (10km walk) will run till he is pulled out.' At the Games, Whitfield won the 800m gold medal, Stone ran bravely to get 6th place in his event, and Laskau was disqualified in his heat of the track walk. As a matter of interest, they were all selected again in 1952. Whitfield successfully defended his title, Stone was 20th in the 10 000m – and Laskau was again disqualified in his heat.

THE MORE THINGS CHANGE, THE MORE THEY ARE THE SAME After the success of the English team at the 1930 British Empire Games at Hamilton, Ontario, an editorial appeared in *The Times* which included comments which might just as aptly be printed today. Consider the following quote: 'Englishmen will probably never be convinced that hurling missiles of various designs, however great the skill required, is equivalent to running once, or twice, or four times round a track. But since a system of differential scoring is not likely to be adopted within two years, they would do well to cultivate throwing disci, putting shot, and hopping, stepping and jumping, before they go to Los Angeles for the next Olympic Games.'

YE ARE MANY, THEY ARE FEW (*Percy Bysshe Shelley*) The largest crowd to watch athletics seems to be one of 132 000 which was at Hampden Park, Glasgow in 1962 to watch a soccer match between Scotland and England. At half-time there was a junior 1 mile race. Similarly at Wembley, London during the FA Cup finals of 1973 and 1974, races were held at half-time in front of a capacity 100 000 spectators. Crowds of about 100 000 have been reported for a Poland v USA athletics match in Warsaw in 1957 and for China v Japan internationals in Beijing in 1979 and 1980.

The greatest attendance at an Olympic stadium purely for athletics was the estimated 100 000 who watched most days of the Games at Berlin in 1936. The Lenin Stadium at Moscow, used for the 1980 Games, held 100 000 but due to the boycott of many Western nations, the audience never exceeded 80 000. The Games at Melbourne in 1956 reached a peak attendance of 91 119, while it is estimated that 90 000 were at the White City Stadium, London during the 1908 Games.

AND IN THIS CORNER The annual Sweden v Finland match was often very physical in its early days (1920s) and unfortunately similar scenes were evident in the 1992 edition in Helsinki. The 1500m event was described as 'a karate match' and the jury unanimously declared the race void.

Perhaps manners and good-sportsmanship in athletics have been overtaken by 'modern living'. Certainly two other unsavoury incidents in 1992 indicate a trend. Firstly there was the unhappy occasion during the Olympic 10 000m when Morocco's Hammou Boutayeb, lapped by the leading runners, attempted to

The annual Sweden v Finland match was often very physical . . .

27

disrupt the running rhythm of Kenya's Richard Chelimo, so aiding his compatriot Khalid Skah to win the title. Then in the world junior championships in Seoul, also in the 10 000m, Josephat Machuka of Kenya gave a violent, bad-tempered push to winner Haile Gebresilasie of Ethiopia just before the line was reached.

LIKE FATHER, LIKE . . .? A study was started in 1992 by students at Glasgow University on the correlation, if any, between a high training mileage (50 miles per week) and the likelihood of fathering daughters instead of sons. Significantly, or perhaps not, both Steve Ovett and Peter McColgan had recently become the proud fathers of baby girls.

THEY FOUR HAD ONE LIKENESS (*Ezekiel*) The first reported relay was an inter-class race run by four men over 2 miles at Berkeley, California in November 1883. It is not known what distance was covered by each runner, but it is likely that it was a medley (e.g. 2 × ¼ mile, 1 × ½ mile, 1 × 1 mile). The first relay using a baton was 'invented' by Frank Ellis and H Geyelin of Pennsylvania in about 1893, and the first relay meeting, the inaugural Penn Relays, was held in 1895. It has been held annually to the present day. The first known relay race in Great Britain was held at Stamford Bridge, London in September 1895, and comprised five teams of three men running a ¼, ¾ and 1 mile respectively. Finchley Harriers were the winners.

BLACK IS BEAUTIFUL At the 1904 Games in St Louis, Joseph Stadler and George Poage, both representing the United States, became the first black men to win medals in Olympic athletics. Stadler won a silver in the standing high jump and Poage took bronzes in the 200m and 400m hurdle races. Four years later in London, their countryman John Taylor gained the first black gold medal as a member of the winning medley relay team. Sadly Taylor, who had qualified as a veterinary surgeon earlier in the year, died of typhoid fever just a few months after his triumph in London.

Considering the large number of black athletes in British teams nowadays, it may be of interest to note that the first to win an Olympic athletics medal for Great Britain was West-Indian born Harry Edward with a 100m bronze in 1920. The first to win a gold medal was Daley Thompson in the decathlon in 1980.

BRINGING HOME THE SALTBEEF The first World Maccabiah Games, for athletes of the Jewish faith, were held in Tel Aviv, then Palestine, in April 1932, when teams from 20 countries participated. The American team was seen off by flamboyant New York Mayor Jimmy Walker with the quip, 'You bring home the bacon – and I'll eat it.' They are now held every four years and about 40 countries are represented.

Usually the American contingents are the largest, but in 1935 there was an exceptionally large team from Germany – many of whom did not return home. The Games are named after Judah Maccabeus, an Israelite hero who drove the Assyrians out of the Temple in Jerusalem in 165 BC.

FIRST COME, FIRST SERVED

James Connolly (USA) was the first athlete to gain a gold medal in the modern Olympic Games when he won the triple jump event in 1896. To be accurate, the event was then named the hop, step and jump, but actually consisted of two hops and then a jump. However, the first athlete to win an Olympic event was another American, Francis Lane, who won the first heat of the 100m about two hours earlier the same day. The first woman to win a gold medal was Helena Konopacka of Poland who took the discus title in July 1928. On the previous day Germany's Anni Holdmann was the inaugural winner of an Olympic women's event when she won heat one of the 100m.

BRITISH WEATHER Perhaps the most unusual case of wind-assistance on record was that which helped set a British 440y mark. Yes, no mistake has been made, a 440y record. It happened at Cardiff during the VIth British Empire & Commonwealth Games in July 1958. The race was a second round heat, held on an extremely blustery day, and England's Ted Sampson ran 0.8 seconds faster than he had ever done before to better the British and European best for the distance.

Knowledgeable spectators reported that the wind seemed to get caught under the stands of Cardiff Arms Park, and swirled around behind the runners for the full circuit of the track. Certainly, Sampson never ran within half a second of the time again and in the semi-final next day was eliminated, clocking a time 1.4 seconds slower. Significantly, all the qualifiers in those second round heats had run faster than expected.

The old White City track was made of cinders which were not very well drained. Many was the occasion, on a typical English summer's day, when the track was inundated, creating conditions which our American and Continental friends rarely experienced. One report made to an overseas publication on one occasion noted that the sprinters not only ran against the wind but also against the tide.

THE GOOD OLD DAYS After the Seoul Olympic Games, just prior to his resignation, Mikhail Gorbachev ordered the Soviet State Sports Committee to cease its support of hundreds of athletes and coaches. No longer would they receive training grants and free medical attention. Apparently, winners at the Seoul Games received a sum of £32 000 (in roubles) plus £785 in hard currency. That sum was estimated to be worth three times Gorbachev's salary.

THEY SHALL NOT PASS By the 1960s the days of big crowds at the White City (of blessed memory) had gone, and at one of the last Oxford v Cambridge matches to be held at the venue there were literally more people competing and officiating than watching. The author and his wife had tickets on the 'posh' side and were feeling quite lonely – and, it must be admitted, somewhat bored – when they noticed two people sitting all alone in the backstraight stand. Binoculars revealed that they were old friends, and a quick stroll round brought us to the entrance to that section of the stand.

Suddenly, a member of the Royal Corps of Commissionaires

appeared, on duty at this point, and asked, quite understandably, to see our tickets. I pointed out that we had much more expensive tickets than were required on this side but wished to sit with our friends.

'I'm sorry, sir, but all these seats are numbered and reserved, and you will have to sit over the other side.' Although I remonstrated with him that there were perhaps 15 000 empty seats on this side, and most certainly nobody else was coming today, he was adamant and rushed off to report us when, I regret to say, we pushed past him. No wonder the

'Don't tell me, let me guess – it's more than your job's worth'

British Army was feared in his day. Soon after this (though not because of it!) the annual match moved away from the White City.

LIES, DAMN LIES AND STATISTICS In 1991 ludicrous predictions were made, by American researchers with little knowledge of the sport, that women would soon match and even surpass men in many events. Showing a much better perception of the realities, the bookmakers William Hill offered odds of 500–1 against a woman holding the overall marathon record by the turn of the century and also 500–1 against a woman holding the 100m record by the year 2050.

This topic, which surfaces every few years or so, fuelled by mathematicians who extrapolate historical data without investigating it thoroughly, is becoming the 'Loch Ness Monster' story of athletics. To put it simply, the problem is that the statistics are not strictly comparable. Men's athletics in modern society goes back to the middle of the 19th century, with widespread competition by the start of the new century. The women's side of the sport did not really begin until the 1920s, and even by the 1950s had not developed into a full programme of events. Thus, taking advantage of the knowledge, techniques and training methods developed by the men, women's records often advanced by leaps and bounds over a very short period. Similarly in recent years, with the advent of female competitors from Africa, India and China – previously barred for various social reasons – standards have shot up.

So when the researchers plot the graphs of women's records against the men's, they note that the rate of increase by the women is often far superior. Then by extrapolating the data forward, the lines cross and the female line rises way ahead of the men. They fail to notice that in the more developed events the two lines are beginning to level off against each other, as one would expect, and that, given the odd hiccup, they will remain that way in the future. Still, such reports make the headlines and the resulting publicity no doubt helps with funding further similar research projects.

ONE THING IS CERTAIN The late Gordon Pirie, arguably Britain's greatest ever distance runner, shared a love–hate relationship with the British press which was rather short on the love side. Pirie was a forthright Yorkshireman who spoke his mind and had no time for false modesty. That was anathema to the media, who rarely lost an opportunity to 'take him down a peg' if they could. The fact that he was the most popular athlete of his time with the athletics public only made the situation worse, as did Pirie himself with often outrageous statements. Thus, when he ran against France in his last international match and won an extremely fast and exciting 5000m, he awaited the press questions quietly.

'When did you think you would win the race?' he was asked.

'When I was selected,' answered Pirie. Some of them never forgave him.

I WANT TO BE ALONE Relations between the Americans and the British at the 1908 Olympic Games in London were not good, with allegations of rule-breaking and fixed heats from the former, and bad manners and bad sportsmanship from the latter. It all came to a head in the final of the 400m in which three of the four finalists were Americans, John Taylor, John Carpenter and William Robbins, and the other a Briton, Wyndham Halswelle. An Army Lieutenant, Halswelle was an experienced athlete, having gained silver and bronze medals in the 1906 400m and 800m respectively, and had set a new Olympic record in his heat. The officials were anticipating trouble in the final, expecting the Americans to 'gang up' on their opponent.

At the gun Robbins shot to the front – there were no lanes in those days – and in so doing appeared to cut across Halswelle, who was inside him at that point, causing him to drop back slightly. Then coming off the bend into the final straight, Carpenter and Halswelle passed Robbins but Carpenter began moving out, seeming deliberately to force the Briton further out, preventing him from passing, while Robbins nipped through on the inside. Irate officials leaped onto the track and broke the finishing tape to void the race. Carpenter was disqualified and a re-run was ordered. Robbins and Taylor refused to run so Halswelle gained the gold medal with the only 'walk-over' in Olympic history.

WE HAVE WAYS The landscaping of the Olympic Stadium surroundings at Munich was created with the rubble caused by Allied bombing of the city during the war. Therefore, at the Games in 1972, it was rather embarrassing to hear one or two Britons loudly claiming that their fathers, presumably in the RAF, had helped build the site.

However, such talk was not all one-sided. One afternoon a group of TV people were talking to the British hurdler Alan Pascoe when the suave and urbane German TV organiser, a former Luftwaffe pilot, happened to come along. Introductions were made, with the added information that Alan came from Portsmouth. 'Ah, yes,' said the German. 'I know it very well – from the air.'

HATS OFF British fans looked forward eagerly to the long-awaited full international match with the Soviet Union in 1956 at the White City. It was going to be the biggest athletics occasion in the United Kingdom since the Wembley Olympics eight years before. Unfortunately, the Soviet team was withdrawn, literally at the last minute, when their record-breaking discus thrower, Nina Ponomaryeva, was accused of attempting to steal hats from an Oxford Street store. Despite the cancellation, hundreds of fans milled around the stadium hoping that there would be a last-minute reprieve for the meeting. Many of them bought what must be an historic programme.

COMMAND OF LANGUAGE There are everyday phrases that can take on whole new meanings when used by a commentator covering international athletics. Thus often there has been the unfortunate description of a triple jumper from a certain Central European country as 'the bouncing Czech'. Similarly, it is so easy to talk about runners from an Eastern bloc neighbour taking 'pole position'. With the entry into top-class athletics of the world's most populous country, the problems

'My receipt? These two
gentlemen are
my receipt'

seem to have multiplied. So it was that on one occasion a competitor from China was described, correctly but in the context unfortunately, as looking 'rather fragile'. However, perhaps the best-remembered example happened during the television report on the 1984 Olympic high jump competition. Noting the inconsistency of the Chinese world record holder reference was made, again correctly, to his nerves being 'the chink in his armour'.

WILSON OF THE WIZARD One often reads that fictional characters have had remarkable influences on people's lives. Within the sport of athletics it is doubtful if many such characters can match the effect that 'Wilson of the Wizard' has had on so many leading figures. *The Wizard* was a boy's comic in the 1930s and 1940s. Unlike the comics of today it was almost totally written material, with just a few drawings, perhaps one per story. Even more unlike today's offerings, it was extremely well written.

One particular character was named Wilson. The basis of the story was very far-fetched. Wilson was born in Yorkshire in 1795, and as a puny child he sought out a famous wise man and learnt how to lead a fit and healthy life. He also learnt the secret of longevity, for in the stories he reappears in 'modern' times – the 1930s – and performs unbelievable feats of running and jumping in the course of his day-to-day activities of helping people.

An amazing number of athletics enthusiasts have admitted that their appetite for the sport was whetted by reading about Wilson. The fact that the stories were wonderfully written, and obviously by a person, or persons,

very knowledgeable about the sport, was an important factor. Although many enquiries have been made, it has never been known for certain who wrote the stories. A number of well-known journalists and writers have been suggested, but none has ever been confirmed. What does seem certain is that the character is based on a composite of a number of well-known athletes of the time, and it is thought that the old-fashioned black running outfit that Wilson always wore was based on the All-Black kit of New Zealand's Jack Lovelock, the 1936 Olympic 1500m champion.

Although most of Wilson's exploits could have been considered ludicrous in the light of the world records of the time, there was always a sneaking suspicion that they were not that impossible. In particular, there was one story which showed amazing foresight.

The author of this book was on an aeroplane going to the European championships at Athens in 1969. Across the aisle was coach Tom McNab, in whose hand luggage I noticed a paperback, a story about Wilson. He allowed me to read it on the journey. It was a compendium of stories, and one was something like 'Wilson and the Pit of Fire'. Wilson was with some companions on the way to an inter-Services meeting in Cairo in the 1940s when his plane was forced to land in the desert. Captured by Bedouins, who had apparently heard of his exploits, he was made to take part in an ancient ritual which entailed leaping over a very long pit of burning coals – a legendary hero had once accomplished it.

In the event Wilson just made it, to great rejoicing by his companions and captors – who had been ready to kill everyone if he failed. One of his friends awoke from a drunken sleep and decided to measure the pit. To his absolute amazement it measured approximately 9.00m (*29ft 6in*) – this at a time when the official world long jump record of 8.13m (*26ft 8¼in*) was hardly ever approached. To me the fascinating thing, as I read the story, was that only the year before the American athlete Bob Beamon had jumped a new world record of 8.90m (*29ft 2½in*), almost exactly the distance that the writer of the Wilson story had predicted some 30 years before.

THE RIGHT NAME Over the years there have been a number of athletes who have rejoiced in a very appropriate name for the event in which they have competed. The most apt surely belonged to the 1936 Olympic long jump silver medallist, Luz Long of Germany. Compatriots of his have included a middle-distance runner named Heinz Laufer (German for runner) and a female high jumper named Springer. The American pole vaulter Dave Volz was the world leader in 1982, while Valto Olenius of Finland won a silver medal in the 1950 European championships in the same event. The best event of New Zealand decathlete Simon Poelman was, coincidentally, the pole vault. In 1992 an American sprinter named James Jett ran a superfast 200m in 19.91, albeit with strong wind assistance (from the jet-stream perhaps?). My own favourite was a New Zealand lady named Phyllis Twidle who threw the discus.

Less appropriate was the name change occasioned by the marriage of Jamaica's Grace Jackson. Jackson, a tall (1.83m), elegant sprinter who won the 1988 Olympic silver medal over 200m, has, on marrying a Jamaican

government official, ironically become Mrs Small. Rather more unusual, and the only known athlete whose name is a palindrome, is Frenchman David Divad, who ran in the 800m at the 1992 World junior championships.

There was an occasion when the 'rightness' of the athlete's name caused problems to the popular BBC commentator Ron Pickering. It was an indoor international match between Great Britain and Spain, and one of the visiting sprinters was named Juan Jones. Now that name is pronounced 'Honesh', but as Ron had once been national coach for Wales the name obviously played on his mind to the extent that when he came to announce the line-up, concentrating his mind so as not to call the Spaniard Jones, he allowed himself to wander, and broadcasting live, he began, 'And in lane Juan . . .'

A FIT COUNTRY FOR HEROES
The first British athlete to actually compete in an Olympic event was Charles Gmelin, who placed fourth in the third 100m heat at Athens in 1896. The first to win an Olympic medal was Grantley Goulding, who gained the silver in the 110m hurdles at the same Games. Charles Bennett, winner of the 1500m at Paris in 1900, was the first Briton to win a gold medal, followed the next day by Alfred Tysoe (800m) and John Rimmer (4000m steeplechase). Linford Christie's 100m win in 1992 brought the British men's gold medal total to 43.

The first British medal won in Olympic women's events, introduced in 1928, was a bronze by the sprint relay team of Eileen Hiscock, Gwen Porter, Violet Webb and Nellie Halstead in 1932 at Los Angeles. Mary Rand (later Toomey) won Britain's first ever women's gold medal at Tokyo in 1964 in the long jump, with a new world record of 6.76 m (*22ft 2¼in*). A few days later Ann Packer (later Brightwell) won the 800m in 2:01.1, also a world record. Since then Britain's women have won only three more events, the 1972 pentathlon by Mary Peters, the 1984 javelin by Tessa Sanderson, and the 1992 400m hurdles by Sally Gunnell.

EVEN STEPHEN Most coaching manuals will tell you that the best and most economical way to run, and win, an 800m race is using even pace. Nowadays that advice is rarely followed, but in the past there were numerous examples of highly successful adherence to the principle. Perhaps the most outstanding was the 1932 Olympic victory by Tom Hampson over more fancied opponents. He ran 400m splits of 54.8 and 54.9 to become the first man in history to break 1:50.0 for the distance.

> ***GEORGE ARMSTRONG CUSTER*** (*apocryphal*)
>
> *'WINNING IS MORE FUN THAN LOSING'*

REMOTE On a recent trip to the remote island of Ascension in the South Atlantic Ocean, renowned athletics researcher Norris McWhirter discovered, to his astonishment, that it contained an athletics track. The island, which is a satellite communications centre, has no permanent population, only the families of the staff. In keeping with the need to make full use of all its 34 square miles, the island church is set within the perimeter of the small cinder track.

> ***PLINY THE ELDER*** (*Roman writer in the 1st century AD*)
>
> *'EX AFRICA SEMPER ALIQUID NOVI (THERE IS ALWAYS SOMETHING NEW OUT OF AFRICA)'*

FIRST OF THE MANY The dominance of East African and particularly Kenyan distance runners has become a fact of athletics life in the 1990s. However, prior to 1954 there was a strong body of opinion, one might say prejudice, which suggested that black runners could not run well at events over 1 mile. The first men to give the lie to this hypothesis were Lazaro Chepkwony and Nyandika Maiyoro, two Kenyans who turned up at the 1954 AAA Championships on their way to the Empire & Commonwealth Games in Vancouver, Canada. Chepkwony, in the 6 miles event, created a stir by running barefoot and setting a very fast pace initially, from the great British runners Pirie, Sando, Norris and Driver. Running far faster than he had ever done before, he paid the penalty just after half-way and dropped out.

Much more impressive was Maiyoro in the 3 miles, and it was undoubtedly his early injection of speed that eventually gave the world record (13:32.2) to Freddie Green and Chris Chataway. He led for about half the race with an effortless, economic style which drew favourable comment from experienced coaches. He then stayed in contention until the last two laps when the Britons struck for home. Maiyoro had won the Kenyan title in 14:04.3, but in the AAA race improved to 13:54.8 for third place.

At the Commonwealth Games, Chepkwony placed seventh in the

6 miles, but the 24-year-old Maiyoro improved still further and placed fourth in the 3 miles with a time of 13:43.8. He appeared in the 1956 Olympics at Melbourne, placing 7th in the 5000m, and improved to sixth in 1960 at Rome. Between those two Olympics their compatriot Arere Anentia gained the first Kenyan medal, a bronze in the 1958 Commonwealth 6 miles in Cardiff, with another Kenyan in sixth place. They were on their way.

It became evident to statisticians that these Kenyans would improve by about 30 seconds on their home 3 mile times and 60 seconds on their 6 mile performances when they ran abroad. At the time it was thought this was due to the better competition and tracks, but what was not realised then was that many of the meetings in Kenya were held at considerable altitude.

Surprisingly, the first championship gold medals won by a Kenyan were for the 100y and 220y, at the 1962 Commonwealth Games at Perth, Australia by Serafino Antao. Antao was of Indian origin so perhaps this 'aberration' does not count. The first gold medals won by what we may term 'African' Kenyans were those won by Kip Keino (1 mile and 3 miles) and Naftali Temu (6 miles) in the Commonwealth Games of 1966 at Kingston, Jamaica. Prior to this the first East African gold medal came at Rome in the 1960 Olympics when the then unknown Abebe Bikila of Ethiopia won the marathon. He won it again in 1964 at Tokyo.

INITIALLY SPEAKING Some years ago the late comedian Kenneth Williams did a brilliant routine involving two civil servants meeting and conversing almost totally in initials (e.g. I'm ADC to the CO of MI5 at the FO, OK?). Within athletics there are times when the unwary passer-by could think that he or she was in the sketch. Below is a brief list of some of the more ubiquitous:

IAAF ..... International Amateur Athletic Federation
AAA ...... Amateur Athletic Association (England)
BAF .... British Athletic Federation
BAAB .... British Amateur Athletic Board (now defunct)
TAC .... The Athletics Congress (USA)
NCAA ... National Collegiate Athletic Association (USA)
WSG ...... World Student Games
OG .... Olympic Games
pb .... personal best
dnf .... did not finish
dnq .... did not qualify
dns .... did not start
qf .... quarter-final
sf .... semi-final
wa .... wind assisted

FROM THE NORTH Rivalling the Kenyans and Ethiopians in the distance events at the end of the 1980s were the North Africans, especially the Moroccans. However, their strength had been in evidence for many years, albeit sometimes disguised by the countries they competed for and the events in which they competed. Perhaps the first noticeable impression made by one of their number was in 1914 when an Algerian, Ahmed Djebellia, won the famous Polytechnic marathon. A fellow countryman, Bougera El Ouafi, came seventh in the 1924 Olympic marathon, but won the gold medal four years later, running both times in the colours of France. A number of other Algerians, Tunisians and Moroccans ran for France over the years, until their countries gained their independence.

The next great Algerian was Alain Mimoun who gained three silver medals for France behind the Czech Emil Zatopek in the 1948 and 1952 Games, before winning the marathon in Melbourne in 1956. Interspersed with these achievements he won the International Cross-Country championship four times. In 1960 that title was won by Rhadi ben Abdessalem, running for Morocco, and he went on that year to gain Morocco's first Olympic medal, a silver in the Rome marathon.

A GOOD LITTLE 'UN Despite the major athletic countries dominating meetings like the Olympic Games and World Championships, the small countries can still make a bid for glory now and then. The outstanding example of this was the unexpected victory of Josy Barthel of Luxembourg in the 1952 Olympic 1500m at Helsinki. At those same Games the island of Jamaica firmly established itself in athletic annals with gold medals in the 400m and 4 × 400m (new world record), and silvers in the 100m, 400m, and 800m. On a *per capita* basis they easily outshone both the United States and the Soviet Union.

Since then, surprisingly, it seems to have become slightly easier for the minnows to beat the sharks. In the 1976 Games Trinidad (Hasely Crawford) and Jamaica (Don Quarrie) won the 100m and 200m respectively. In the World Championships, Eamonn Coghlan of Ireland won the 5000m in 1983, Somalia's Abdi Bile took the 1500m in 1987, and Samuel Matete of Zambia won the 400m hurdles

in 1991. Other 'small' nations to be successful at this high level have been Norway, Portugal, Algeria and Uganda. At the time of writing there were 203 countries affiliated to the governing body of the sport (IAAF) and the bulk of them are beginning to produce high-class athletes.

INFORMING THE PUBLIC An article in the London *Evening Standard* in February 1992 about sex-testing referred to 'the East German sisters Tamara and Irina Press' retiring prematurely 'from international swimming'. One wonders in which events the Soviet sisters took part, especially the 95kg Tamara. In fact, of course, she won Olympic titles in the shot (1960–64) and discus (1964), while her sister won the 80m hurdles (1960) and the pentathlon (1964), pushing Mary Rand back to second place in the latter.

SOME CORNER OF A FOREIGN FIELD Quite a number of British athletics heroes of the past were born abroad. Unlike today, when immigration has strengthened British teams immeasurably, these cases were due primarily to their parents being abroad for religious, diplomatic, military or business purposes. Into the first of these categories fits the 1924 Olympic 400m champion Eric Liddell, born in China of missionary parents. Half of Britain's victorious 4 × 400m team in 1936 were born abroad, Godfrey Brown in India and Freddie Wolff in Hong Kong.

Following that pattern later were Olympic relay silver medallists Robbie Brightwell and David Jenkins. Brightwell was born in India and Jenkins in Trinidad, and both won European 400m titles in

1962 and 1971 respectively. The 1956 Olympic steeplechase champion Chris Brasher was born in what is now Guyana (then British Guiana) and Ken Wilmshurst, the 1954 Commonwealth long and triple jumps gold medallist, was born in India. Bill Tancred, who has held the British discus record since 1974 and gained a silver medal in that year's Commonwealth Games, was born in Quetta, now Pakistan.

Of course, other countries have also benefited from foreign-born recruits especially the United States, whose generous immigration policies have rewarded them with many fine athletes, notably from Ireland and the West Indies. However, perhaps their most famous such athlete was Frank Shorter who won the Olympic marathon in 1972 in the city of his birth, Munich. Another famous Olympian was Irena Szewinska, who won three gold, two silver, and three bronze medals for Poland from 1964 to 1976 but was actually born in Leningrad, USSR.

FOOTPRINTS IN THE SAND OF TIME (*Henry Wadsworth Longfellow*) The longest lasting British record in a standard Olympic event was Irishman Peter O'Connor's long jump of 7.61m (*24ft 11¾in*) which remained unbeaten for 59 years 9 days from when it was set in August 1901. The equivalent best in a track event is the 200m (actually 220y) time of 21.2 by Willie Applegarth set in July 1914, which withstood attacks for 44 years and 92 days. It should be noted, however, that Walter George's famous mile time of 4:12.75 in August 1886, when he was a professional, was not surpassed by a Briton until Sydney Wooderson ran 4:12.7 in August 1935, 48 years 345 days later.

The longevity record for a standard world mark, also in the long jump, is the 25 years 79 days that it took to better Jesse Owens' performance of 8.13m (*26ft 8¼in*) set in May 1935. Also worth noting is the unofficial clocking of 10.2 in a 110y race in June 1921 by the then Olympic champion Charlie Paddock (USA). That time was not beaten over 100m for 29 years 111 days. Note must also be taken of the outstanding mile by Walter George, mentioned above, which was not beaten by an amateur until Norman Taber (USA) ran 4:12.6 in July 1915, nearly 29 years later.

Records in non-standard events often lasted for exceptional periods. Thus, the longest duration for an official IAAF running world record is 35 years 39 days for the 15-mile time of 1hr20:04.6 set by Fred Appleby (GB) in July 1902. The no longer recognised 20 mile walk record stood to Thomas Griffith (GB) for 61 years 129 days from December 1870 when he clocked 2hr47:52 for the event.

Currently the longest extant world record is the undoubtedly altitude-assisted 19.72 for 200m by Pietro Mennea of Italy, set at Mexico City in September 1979.

IT'S SUPERMAN One of the most startling athletic performances ever achieved was the 20km record set by the phenomenal Czech runner Emil Zatopek in September 1951. To set the scene, one must realise that up to that date only five men in history had run 10km in a sub-30 minutes time, while Zatopek's world mark was 29:02.6. Two of those, Heino and Maki of Finland, were the previous world record holders for the distance and were no longer operational. The other three had only just slipped under the half-hour. Thus the news that Zatopek had run two consecutive sub-30 minutes, to clock 59:51.8 for the 20km distance, was quite staggering to all aficionados of the sport.

THE DREAMING SPIRES OF UXBRIDGE In a tribute to Gordon Pirie, the *Irish Runner* magazine of February 1992 noted that 'he was a star from the working classes and not from Uxbridge.' Since there were also references to Pirie's contemporaries, Bannister and Chataway, one assumes that the mythical place they meant was Oxbridge (the combination of Oxford and Cambridge) and not the area in Middlesex which was home from home for most of the competitors at the London Olympics of 1948.

TALL AS A TREE The tallest ever international-class athlete is shot putter Karsten Stolz of Germany who stands 2.08m (*6ft 10in*). With a best putt of 21.15m, he has won his national title on four occasions and twice placed second in the European Indoor championships. Britain's tallest ever international athlete is high jumper Geoff Parsons who measures 2.03m (*6ft 8in*). He jumped 2.30m in 1990 and won the AAA title three times.

EXCUSE ME, MISS? The scourge of sport in the last half of the 20th century has been the taking of steroids and other drugs. One of the few humorous stories to emerge from an otherwise very serious matter is the one about the male thrower who, asked to provide a sample for testing, endeavoured to substitute one from his girlfriend in place of his own. When the results came through, he was pronounced clean – but pregnant!

'I hear congratulations are in order'

FINLANDIA The domination of the distance track events by Finnish runners in the 1920s and 1930s has never been matched, not even by the Kenyans in the 1980s. This supremacy, and one cannot really call it anything less, actually began in 1912. The first of the 'Flying Finns' was Johannes Kolehmainen who won the 5000m, 10000m and the 12km cross-country event at Stockholm, also leading his team to a silver in the latter race. He returned in 1920 to win the marathon but was now beginning to be overshadowed by Paavo Nurmi, who took the 10000m and the 8km cross-country, with the Finnish team also taking gold in the latter. Nurmi added a silver in the 5000m.

In 1924 at Paris they really took over, with Nurmi winning the 5000m (and the 1500m for good measure on the same afternoon) and leading his team to victories in the 10km cross-country and 3km team races, coming first in both. His great rival Ville Ritola won gold in the 10000m and the 3000m steeplechase, and took second place in both the 5000m and the cross country. Finns also took silver in the steeplechase and bronze in the 10000m. Albin Stenroos topped it all off with a win in the marathon. Ironically, the Swede Edwin Wide, who split the Finns to get a silver in the 10000m and a bronze in the 5000m, was born in Finland.

At Amsterdam in 1928 Harri Larva won the 1500m, with a team-mate in third, while Ritola won the 5000m and Nurmi the 10000m. The former also gained a silver in the 10000m and Nurmi got silvers in the 5000m and steeplechase. That event was won by Toivo Loukola with a team-mate in third, so making a clean sweep. Another bronze was picked up in the marathon. Old rival Wide placed third in both the 5000m and 10000m.

The tragedy of 1932 was the disbarring of Nurmi for irregularities with expenses on a foreign tour. He was as near certain a favourite for the marathon as anyone could be. Nevertheless, in his absence Lauri Lehtinen won the 5000m with Lauri Virtanen in third place. Volmari Iso-Hollo took the steeplechase and placed second in the 10000m, while Armas Toivonen won the bronze medal in the marathon.

The Finnish Olympic swan-song came in 1936. In the 10000m Ilmari Salminen led a 1–2–3 ahead of Arvo Askola and Iso-Hollo, while the latter successfully defended his steeplechase title with Finns in

second and fourth places. The 5000m gold medal was won by Gunnar Hockert with Lehtinen placed second.

There is good reason to believe that more gold medals would have been forthcoming in the Games of 1940 and 1944 had they been held, with the likes of Taisto Maki and Viljo Heino more than capable of upholding the great traditions of their predecessors. However, by 1948 the ravages of war had left the reservoir depleted and it was not until the 1970s that Finnish Olympic pride was reborn in the shape of Lasse Viren.

During the period 1912 to 1940 the various 'Flying Finns' set over 70 world records of one sort or another in the events ranging from 1500m to the marathon, a unique record in itself.

SMALL IS BEAUTIFUL Almost certainly the smallest athlete to win a major championship was Annerita Sidoti of Italy, the 1990 European women's 10km walk gold medallist. At the time of her victory she was only 1.50m (*4ft 11in*) tall. A possible contender for the title is Akemi Matsuno of Japan, who placed second in the 1992 Osaka marathon and is one of her country's major prospects. She is only 1.48m (*4ft 10¼in*) and weighs a mere 35½kg (*78lb*).

THE MOSTEST When Sergei Bubka, formerly of the Soviet Union and now of the Ukraine, pole vaulted 6.15m (*20ft 2¼in*) at Donetsk on 21 February 1993, it was the 34th time that he had set a world mark for the event. This total comprised 16 outdoor records and 18 indoors since 1984. That is far in excess of anything previously achieved in one event. The legendary Finn Paavo Nurmi was credited with 29 outdoor records in 16 different events from 1500m to 20km between 1924 and 1931. In addition he set another 6 indoor marks. The most records set by a woman is 26, including 10 indoors, by Marita Koch (GDR) at events from 50m to 400m between 1977 and 1985. The most by a woman in one event was 18, including 4 indoors, by Iolanda Balas of Romania in the high jump between 1956 and 1961.

Middle-distance ace Gundar Haegg of Sweden in 1942, and Australian distance star Ron Clarke in 1965, both set a record 10 world records in a year, but at various events. The most in a single event is 8 in the women's high jump by Iolanda Balas (Romania) in 1961, of which half were indoors. This was matched by Sergei Bubka in the pole vault in 1991. The best for a solely outdoor event was by Gisela Mauermayer of Germany in 1935 when she improved the world discus mark seven times.

SUCCINCTLY PUT The only British runner to win the famous New Year's Eve race in Sao Paulo, Brazil, is Ken Norris in 1956. The race, then 7300m (*4½ miles*) in length, is always affected by heat, humidity, car fumes, cobbled roads and general confusion. That year the race was particularly tough and Norris had very little left as he staggered over the line, only to have a microphone shoved in his face. In answer to the inevitable question of how he felt, he gave one of the shortest, pithiest answers ever by an athlete in such a situation. 'Bloody,' he said. Ken can now be seen working for TV on the infield of stadia around Britain.

IN AND OUT At the 1970 NCAA championships in America held at Des Moines, Iowa, world records were set both indoors and outdoors. The latter record was for the 440y hurdles, in which Ralph Mann clocked 48.8. Not long after that performance a torrential rainstorm occurred, resulting in the pole vault being moved indoors. During this competition the formerly unheralded Jan Johnson cleared 5.36m (*17ft 7in*) which bettered the indoor record.

PLAYING THE PERCENTAGES The eminent athletics statistician Peter Matthews has calculated that the greatest percentage improvement in an IAAF men's world record was 6.59% by Bob Beamon's long jump of 8.90m (*29ft 2½in*) at the Mexico City Olympics in 1968. However, he also notes that prior to official records, the Swede Eric Lemming improved the javelin mark by 10.83% with a throw of 49.32m (*161ft 10in*) in 1899.

SUMMON UP THE BLOOD (*Henry V*) In the last 10 years there have been repeated accusations that a number of athletes, and particularly some from Italy, have been involved in what is termed 'blood-doping'. Simply put, this is the act of having blood removed and stored, under appropriate conditions, while the body replenishes the loss. Then the original blood is reintroduced into the body, thus increasing its oxygen-carrying capacity. At a Press conference prior to a GB v Italy match the Promotions Officer of British athletics, Andy Norman, apologising for the lack of stars in the Italian team, commented, no doubt tongue in cheek, that there was some 'new blood' in their team.

New Year's Eve in Sao Paulo

Jogger attacked by stationary lamp-post

44

THINGS THAT GO BUMP A survey of its readers by *Running* magazine in 1992 indicated that the greatest hazard to training on the roads was that caused by inanimate objects. It was quite remarkable how often parked cars, walls, builder's scaffolding and lamp-posts made unprovoked attacks on innocent runners. Other vicious assailants included bus shelters, trees and park benches. Apparently, motorists were not as serious a problem as had been thought, although a reader reported one who 'gave me a short ride on the bonnet'. Not surprisingly, some 61% of the surveyed had been attacked by dogs.

AGE SHALL NOT WITHER THEM Ever since the emergence of the superb runners from East Africa there have been doubts expressed about their quoted ages. The Ethiopian 1980 double Olympic champion Miruts Yifter (dubbed 'Yifter the Shifter') was said to be anything between 34–41 years of age. In more recent times his countryman Addis Abebe won the 1988 World Junior 10 000m title, despite being referred to by a famous TV commentator as 'looking the oldest teenager I have ever seen'. A probable reason for these discrepancies is that there is a difference between the Ethiopian calendar and the European one of 7 or 8 years.

Not so simply explained are the variances in the dates of birth of many of the Kenyan youngsters on the world scene. It is understood that their ages are determined by the birthdate shown on their passports, a totally acceptable routine in most of the world. However, it transpires that it is very easy to get a Kenyan passport – one merely has to provide the authorities with a document from your doctor noting your date of birth. Thus, it is not difficult to apply for another passport should you want to establish a different age. Reasons for being of different ages are not difficult to find for aspiring runners. Entry to international junior competitions opens up untold opportunities; being too old limits job opportunities in government agencies; and recruitment to an American university usually depends on being fairly young.

Statisticians have been run ragged by African dates of birth especially, and the acknowledged expert on African athletics recently confessed to finding his age data an embarrassment. More importantly, the domination of world junior titles in the distance events by East African runners loses some significance in the light of the above.

THIS MUST BE THE PLACE The athletics track which has been the venue of most world records is the Stockholm Olympic stadium, which was inaugurated in May 1912. It was designed and laid by Charles Perry, the Englishman who also laid out the old White City track. Although altered over the years the stadium still looks the same outwardly. By the end of 1992 there had been a total of 123 world marks set there, comprising 110 by men and 13 by women. Its nearest rival among existing stadia is the Los Angeles Coliseum with 103.

The city which has hosted most records is London with 195, of which the larger number (115) have been by women. Of that total, 109 were at the old White City, built originally for the 1908 Olympic Games.

AS THE SAYING GOES

IAN STEWART (1970 Commonwealth 5000m champion – to *Athletics Weekly* 1975)

'First is first and second is nowhere. You race to win. If you're not running to win you may as well pack up. It's no more acceptable to finish second by half a stride than it is to finish last, just because they give you a medal for it. If we took away the second and third medal and said only the winner gets a medal, see how everybody feels about it then'

LEWIS CARROLL (Queen of Hearts in *Alice's Adventures in Wonderland*)

'Now, here, you see, it takes all the running you can do, to keep in the same place. If you want to get somewhere else, you must run at least twice as fast as that'

PETE ROSE (*American baseball player – on speed around the bases*)

'I'M NOT A GREAT RUNNER. BUT I'M NOT BAD FOR A WHITE GUY'

LIZ McCOLGAN (1991 World 10 000m champion – prior to defeat in 1992 World Cross-Country championships)

'If you can't take losing you shouldn't be in sport. I think I'm one of the best in the world, but I'm not invincible'

DEREK REDMOND (British 400m record holder – after his fifth Achilles operation)

'It got to the point where I asked the surgeon if he was going to put zips in'

ANN PACKER (discussing her 1964 Olympic 800m triumph)

'You feel the responsibility of feeling people want you to do well. You're aware of all those things. It's really a relief. The fear of losing is pretty strong'

IAN STEWART (former running great – answering mocking comments about his wearing an old Birchfield vest in 1992 National Road Relay)

'I've had this vest since I was fifteen. This vest has run faster than you, Milovsorov, and my attitude is that if it was good enough when I was running fast, then I'll wear it when I'm running – – – – – – – slow'

STEVE OVETT (on the 1976 Olympic 800m final – he finished fifth)

'They ran the first lap in lanes. By the time they broke there was a guy twenty yards in front (Juantorena). It didn't even give me a chance to say goodbye to him'

AVERY BRUNDAGE (former President of the IOC – answering American 'hysteria' about Soviet state-aided athletes in 1956)

'Champions are not made by subsidies or training camps, but by diligence and intelligence. It is not the strength of other people that we in the United States need fear. It is our natural complacency and the softness of life brought on by too much prosperity. The fact that the complaints have come from a country that has been

notorious for gross irregularities in sport at educational institutions has not added to their validity and, I am sorry to say, they sound like sour grapes to the rest of the world'

DANNY EVERETT (Olympic 4 × 400m relay gold medallist – discussing the 1991 World championship relay)

'I think Pettigrew underestimated the pressure that goes with being anchor, the pressure that goes with being close, and he underestimated someone just because they hadn't run under 44.5sec . . . But it doesn't translate like that. If it did we wouldn't have to run relays. We would just take the four fastest times, put them together and let that be that'

DAVID BEDFORD (talking in 1992 about the new British team manager Joan Allison)

'She does have one weakness. She can only carry one filing cabinet at a time'

SEBASTIAN COE (prior to the Moscow Olympics)

'I go to Moscow totally committed. If I lose I'll be pretty choked for a couple of days, but life does go on'

(Coe lost the 800m final on 26 July, but won the 1500m on 1 August)

VLADIMIR KUTS (Soviet 1956 Olympic 10 000m gold medallist – about Gordon Pirie of Great Britain who had made a race of it)

'I had done everything I could to shake off that shadow. I was desperately tired and ready to surrender, and then I

thought that before I did, I had to see his face, not his shadow. So I moved out into the second lane, offering him the lead, and I looked into his face. If I had seen a flicker of triumph, the race would have been his, but I saw only pain and I knew that the race was mine'

CHRIS CHATAWAY (reminiscing about his 5000m world record in 1954)

'I remember that – it was the nearest thing to being dead I have ever experienced'

AGK 'GODFREY' BROWN (Olympic relay gold medallist 1936)

'The strongest man in the finish of a 400m race is not the one who accelerates the most, but rather the one who decelerates the least'

OLGA BONDARENKO (Soviet 1988 Olympic 10 000m champion – in *Athletics Weekly*, December 91)

'Winning world or European titles or making money on the Grand Prix circuit are not important to me. The only thing that matters is winning Olympic gold'

ANDY NORMAN (British athletics promotions officer – on the poor state of women's athletics in Britain)

'Our women have been given the same opportunities but they always seem to have a problem in the last 24 hours. The goldfish has drowned or their coach says that they've got to save themselves for the League the following weekend'

Zatopek's coach irons out a few technical faults

EMIL ZATOPEK (1952 Olympic 5000m/10 000/marathon winner – asked why he grimaced)

'I am not talented enough to run and smile at the same time'

ABEL KIVIAT (1500m world record holder in 1912, speaking at age 98 in 1990)

'Today's runners run more in a week than I did in a year'

LYNN JENNINGS (after winning the World Cross-Country title for the third time in 1992)

'Cross-country at the international level can be like that. I'm used to the pushing and shoving – you have to stake your place on the corners – that's all part of it'

GODFREY RAMPLING (British gold medallist 1936 Olympic 4 × 400m relay)

'The great difference I see is that what we did we did for fun. We made nothing out of it, and we just ran because we liked running'

LISA YORK (1992 English National Cross-Country champion)

'Bud Baldaro (her coach) reckons I have the concentration powers of a goldfish'

THOMAS OSANO (Kenyan road-racing ace)

'I always like racing hills, because that is my way of life – uphill'

'An unusually large crowd has gathered for the high jump here today . . .'

SANDRA FARMER-PATRICK (American 400mH record holder – on her eye-catching running outfits)

'The short chiffon skirt is not an aerodynamic handicap. It adds femininity and flair. Of course, it's not for everybody. High jumpers wouldn't wear it'

TRACK & FIELD NEWS (on Farmer-Patrick after she won at Lausanne in 1991)

'Farmer-Patrick made a slow tour of the stadium, while blowing kisses to the fans. At the completion of the lap she ripped off her chiffon dress, revealing a skimpy bikini brief. If only Gypsy Rose Lee had tried the hurdles . . .'

TIM HUTCHINGS (British distance star – talking about his injury in 1992)

'I think one of the benefits of having a long-term injury is knowing that you can have a glass of beer or that extra piece of pudding. Whereas before there is always that pressure on you to watch your diet, get to bed early, save your energy for the next day's training. That's a constant pressure that most people don't see. Basically, I've become a more normal human being'

THE AUTHOR (to Sebastian Coe, at the Middlesex championships May 1985)

'It's a lovely day – pity to waste it'

(Coe then ran a remarkable 800m in 1:44.0, winning by 7 seconds)

ROGER BANNISTER (first 4-minute miler)

'I sometimes think that running has given me a glimpse of the greatest freedom that a man can ever know, because it results in the simultaneous liberation of both body and mind'

ROGER BLACK (European/Commonwealth 400m champion, in June 1992)

'I don't take offence if people think I might be on drugs. Unfortunately, because of what's happened in the sport you start suspecting anybody who's doing particularly well. I suspect certain people, too, so why should I be excluded from other people's suspicions?'

LISA ONDIEKI (on the attitude of her husband Yobes, the 1991 World 5000m champion)

'Yobes told me he didn't look at his lap times in Tokyo. He told me he ran until he couldn't hear anyone. He went out to run the field off their legs. By comparison I'm just a nice, Western, conservative-thinking runner. I'll always finish in the top three. At times Yobes will do something crazy in a race and he'll blow up. But it's the difference between doing something really great, or just being another good runner. He has taught me if I want to do something great, I've got to be willing to let go and just run'

ANDY NORMAN (British athletics promotions officer)

'The difference between being a good athlete and the best in the world is very minute. Generally, it is a state of mind'

LIZ McCOLGAN

'Sometimes I think the day I hang up my running shoes will be the day that my life really begins'

NICK OWEN (British television anchorman during the 1988 Olympics)

'And now from one Joyner to another – Peter Elliott'

(At the time Peter Elliott was a carpenter)

CARL LEWIS (on not doing four events in the 1992 Olympic Games)

'Let's say I do the 100m, 200m and long jump. I've got world record holder Mike Powell waiting in the long jump; Leroy Burrell in the 100m, and Michael Johnson in the 200m. All those people focus on one event. I have to split everything and it takes something away from each event, no matter how good you are. I've inspired everyone and they've caught up because they've specialised'

LIZ McCOLGAN (on her 1991 World title)

'It was so hard to go out and win the big one. It's easy to be one of the best runners in the world, but to actually go out and win the championship proves it to everyone'

JOSE LUIS BARBOSA (Brazilian 800m runner, in late 1991)

'I feel very good and not at all tired. It's just that I can't relax. I want so badly to run a really good time but the clock is blocking me. It's my body against the clock and so far the clock has won'

ROGER BLACK (again on people who suspect him of drug abuse)

'In a strange way I take it as a compliment, because it implies that the quality of my performances – which I know to be genuine – could have been brought about only by these means. It has become part of the job nowadays to be under suspicion, a case of guilt by association'

ALBERTO JUANTORENA (powerful (1.91m tall) Cuban Olympic 400m/800m champion, on his plans to move up in distance)

'I hear those little milers like to bump each other. Somehow I don't think they will bump me'

LEE EVANS (1968 Olympic 400m champion – asked about the dearth of white sprinters)

'There are white guys who could run faster than me, only they're too busy making money on Wall Street'

ANNOUNCER (at Crystal Palace during GB v Germany match, June 1991)

'With that result computed – hah, computed! I'm using an envelope and a biro – the score now is . . .'

DENIS POTTER (dramatist and critic)

'At Crystal Palace the BBC cameras picked up a solemn lady as she pounded along a running track with "British Meat" written across her understandably heaving bosom. Sponsorship in sport is one thing but this was altogether a different kettle of offal'

BABE DIDRIKSON (US track star of the 1930s – about athletics judges)

'They're stupid. All you have to do to win if it's close is throw up your arm just before the finish, and they think you're first'

EMIL ZATOPEK (Czech triple Olympic champion in 1952)

'For me a day without a visit to a track is like a meal without wine or a day without sun'

FANNY BLANKERS-KOEN (Dutch quadruple Olympic champion 1948)

'All I have done is run fast. I don't quite see why people should make so much fuss about that'

LINFORD CHRISTIE (Olympic, European and Commonwealth sprint champion)

'I never train like a champion. I always train like a contender'

JESSE OWENS (winner of 4 gold medals at 1936 Olympics – on being black)

'I was not invited to shake hands with Hitler, but I was not invited to the White House to shake hands with the President either'

KRISS AKABUSI (British 400m hurdles record holder)

'Without a doubt my upbringing has been critical. One of the things I've always wanted to prove is that I'm as good as they are, and that I'm not just some kid from a children's home. Sport was the ideal way because no matter who you are, when you get on that track everyone's equal. You all dance to the same tune and fortunately I've danced better than most'

GISELA MAUERMAYER (1936 Olympic discus champion – as a zoologist in 1972)

'As a zoologist I can attest by scientific tests that no animal exists which can sustain the kind of effort demanded nowadays by a high-performance athlete'

OATH-TAKER AT AN OLYMPIC GAMES (on behalf of all competitors)

'In the name of all competitors, I promise that we will take part in these Olympic Games, respecting and abiding by the rules which govern them, in the true spirit of sportsmanship, for the glory of sport and the honour of our teams'

AP HERBERT (rhapsodising about Soviet distance ace Vladimir Kuts)

'Vladimir, Vladimir, Vladimir Kuts, Nature's attempt at an engine in boots'

FATHER HENRI DIDON (composed in 1895, the last part became the Olympic motto in 1920)

'Here is your watchword – Citius, Altius, Fortius (Faster, Higher, Stronger)'

BARON PIERRE DE COUBERTIN (based on words used in a sermon by the Bishop of Pennsylvania at St Paul's, London, in 1908)

'The most important thing in the Olympic Games is not to win but to

take part, just as the most important thing in life is not the triumph but the struggle. The essential thing is not to have conquered but to have fought well'

GWENDA WARD (referring to Sally Gunnell's British record win in the 1991 Monte Carlo Grand Prix)

'The performance was totally undervalued by the Press. Steve Cram, who came fourth in his race the same night, got more coverage for merely consolidating his place in the team. This blatant unfairness has nothing to do with the 'inferiority' of

the women's performances and everything to do with male journalists and editors' vague notions of what is newsworthy, which is never subjected to objective scrutiny'

GERRY HELME (agent for some Kenyan runners – on the problem of too many Kenyans in European cross-country races)

'It's the meeting director's responsibility to limit the amount of Kenyans they allow into their races . . . Even if you only have one Kenyan in the field though, he may run away with it – but you can't legislate for that'

No room on the back page for Sally

SIR ARTHUR GOLD (former chairman of the British Olympic Association)

'The ancient Olympics survived for 1100 years before it was destroyed by money and politics – and they say the one thing that man learns from history is that he doesn't learn'

STEPHEN BAGLEY (newspaper columnist)

'Of all the possible solecisms, vulgarisms and errors of taste which consumer civilisation provides, there is none so profound or unsettling as athletic shoes on the pot-bellied'

PRIMO NEBIOLO (IAAF President in 1991 – prior to the voting on readmission of South Africa to the Federation)

'I don't have the vote in my pocket, but I am sure the answer will be yes'

CHRIS BRASHER (1956 Olympic steeplechase champion and sports journalist)

'There is little doubt that an athlete in training ceases to be a normal being'

BILL COSBY (American comedian and former college athlete)

' "Relay" means you are no longer an individual. "Relay" means you must learn to share and alter behaviour. "Relay" means you have to do your part above and beyond what you expect of yourself'

BRUCE TULLOH (the former European 5000m champion puts running in a new light when he quotes Woody Allen's remarks about sex)

'It's the most fun you can have without laughing'

DICK JOHNSON (Australian supporter writing about the travel problems facing fans at the 1992 Olympic Games in Barcelona)

'I feel that in some ways those spectators who attended all track and field sessions had to be in better condition than some of the athletes. I'm not sure that I peaked at the right time'

CHRIS CHATAWAY (asked his reaction to little-known winner of 1954 European 5000m title, Vladimir Kuts)

'It was a most appalling shock when he did not come back'

GORDON PIRIE (looking back on his career and unrelenting training schedule)

'I have run a phenomenal mileage, and the only thing I have learned from that is don't, because when you do your greatest mileage you have the worst results'

QUINCY WATTS (1992 Olympic 400m champion)

'Success and hard work comes from the backbone and not the wishbone. You can wish this and wish that, but when it comes down to it, it's all about backbone'

BENSON MASYA (Kenyan half-marathon world record holder – on the reason he gave up boxing)

'Because my feet are faster than my hands'

PETER McCOLGAN (when anaemia had been diagnosed in wife Liz after the 1992 Olympics)

'The problem with any athlete is that they are the last people to know when they're in shape'

JAVIER GARCIA (surprise Spanish 1992 Olympic pole vault bronze medallist)

'I want to thank the crowd for their constant support, it really helped me; but I didn't like the way they booed my rivals. This is athletics, not football'

ROGER BLACK (about his surprising decision to run the first leg on the winning world championship relay)

'I could have said I wanted the last leg. They couldn't have taken it away from me. But I knew it was right I went on the first leg and I would do it again – even if it meant the ego had to be put away'

JOHN DOWNES (Irish cross-country runner referring to Kenyan victories in the 1991/92 winter)

'If you make the Kenyans run backwards they would still run faster than anyone else'

DEREK REDMOND (British 400m record holder – after a rather poor effort in his first indoor 800m in January 1992)

'I take tennis lessons, but that doesn't mean I'm going to enter Wimbledon'

KIM McDONALD (agent for numerous Kenyan runners – on the problem of too many Kenyans running and winning in Europe)

'There are many athletes in Kenya who are interested in coming to Europe, who are as good, if not better, than the ones already on the circuit'

STEVE OVETT (on the 1980 Olympic 800m final – he finished first)

'It was a very physical race. There were some guys in there bouncing off me. I didn't run into guys deliberately. Guys came across me and they found I was perhaps a lot stronger than they thought, and they just bounced off me'

ANDY NORMAN (British athletics promotion officer)

'Top women athletes are stars in the world – the achievers plus the lookers, Merlene Ottey, Katrin Krabbe. But if you look at some of the Russian ladies who've won gold medals, you wouldn't even know their names'

PAUL EVANS (British runner – on proliferation of Kenyans in British road races)

'You go to a race, someone opens a minibus, and they all fall out. It

*Tom's educational
video nasty*

doesn't matter where you go they are there in their droves. You can go to France and there will be 15 to 20 of them'

TIM HUTCHINGS (World Cross-Country silver medallist – on the dominance of the Kenyan runners)

'You almost begin to wonder whether there should be an African cross-country championships, and the rest of the world'

MALCOLM JONES (chief executive of the British Athletic Federation – on coming into the sport of athletics)

'Once you get into it, it starts to engross you. It takes you over. You get more and more involved, and it takes over your life'

JOHN MAYOCK (young middle-distance runner – on his training mileage)

'I try to get away with as little as I possibly can, so there is plenty of room for improvement. I know there are runners the same age as me who are already doing 100 miles per week. But if I did that there would be nothing left for the future'

TOM McKEAN (1990 European 800m champion)

'I have all my disasters on video and I watch them all frequently, because you only learn from losing races, and I don't see any point in hiding from them'

ANDY NORMAN (British promotions officer, talking about agent John Bicourt's house, often full of Kenyan clients)

'Actually the Kenyan High Commission is really in Auckland Road, Crystal Palace'

CARINA GRAHAM (outspoken veteran athlete)

'I am not an elitist but resent people who do not train regularly, are unfit, inept, just turn up and drop the hammer or shot on their toes. I don't agree, either, that it doesn't matter if you come last. Like hell it matters, to an athlete, any real competitor'

LAURA THOMPSON (*The Times* columnist, reflecting on Britain's poor early showing at 1991 world championships)

'An athletics career can be built upon lots of training, lots of parading, hands on hips, an appearance on A Question of Sport, an occasional great run at Crystal Palace and lots of excuses'

PETER NICHOLS (editor of the *Guinness Sports Yearbook* – on the probable readmittance of South Africa to the IAAF in 1992)

'There is no sporting or even political currency involved. It's all about the driving ambition of one man'

DAVID BEDFORD (former distance running great – on his lifestyle in 1992)

'Then I spring down to the station –

waddle is probably a better word –
which thankfully is only about 500
yards from home'

JOHN BICOURT (athletes' agent
and former steeplechase
international)

'Telling an athlete what he's worth
can create problems. Some don't

understand the practicalities and think
they're worth more than they are'

TRACK & FIELD NEWS (in a
1991 report on the decline of
athletics – track & field in
American parlance – in the United
States)

'What if they gave a track meet and
nobody came?'

FASTER THAN THE SPEEDING BULLET

CARL LEWIS (about Santa Monica Track Club coach Tom Tellez)

'Coach T demands perfection. Most coaches don't demand you to be perfect. They mask it with emotion. Here, there is only one way to run and that's the right way. Period. End of discussion. If you make a mistake, you work on that mistake. When you correct that mistake, you run faster'

EDDIE HART (won 1972 US Olympic Trials 100m in 9.9 – first sprinter to wear 'shades' while running)

'Man, I'm so fast I need them for re-entry'

LINFORD CHRISTIE (1992 Olympic 100m champion)

'I have no friends in sprinting because I train so hard it hurts; and when the season starts they will all pay for the pain, the celibacy and everything else I put myself through'

TOM TELLEZ (coach – to Carl Lewis prior to 1991 World championship 100m)

'You ran your best race in the Rome world championships in the semis. You ran your best race in the Seoul Olympics in the semis. I will not have you run your best race in the damn semis here'

(He didn't – WR 9.86 in the final)

SAM MUSSABINI (coach – to Harold Abrahams prior to 1924 Olympic 100m final)

'Only think of two things: the report of the gun and the tape. When you hear the one, just run like hell until you break the other'

LINFORD CHRISTIE (prior to Barcelona – about his age)

'The only significance it would have for me is that I'd be able to shut up half the British press. They were always saying that I was too old. That would be the only pleasure, because then I could turn round and blow a raspberry'

JOHN COOK (US track coach – about racial stereotyping)

'It's like asking why can't American white kids sprint. They can't sprint because they won't sprint'

TOM TELLEZ (coach – to Carl Lewis after 1984 Olympic 100m victory)

'Yeah, you won. But you didn't have a good start'

JOHN DRUMMOND (on splitting his pants winning the 1991 World Student Games 200m title)

'That's what I call running, when you run out of your clothes'

KEVIN LITTLE (American white sprinter – third in 1989 World Indoor 200m)

'It's intimidating when your the only white. People go "What's he doing out there?" I felt intimidated until I proved I could beat the majority of these guys. Now that I have confidence in my ability, it doesn't even cross my mind I'm the only white out there'

DENNIS MITCHELL (prior to 1992 Olympic trials)

'Saying "I'm going to Barcelona" is like spending more money than you actually have. You don't have a credit card in track; you have to pay cash wherever you go'

EVELYN ASHFORD (1984 Olympic 100m champion – on post-Olympic gold trauma)

'You think there's going to be this elated joy, because you're looking for it. But it doesn't happen. It was certainly enjoyable winning though'

KATHARINE MERRY (British junior champion on 1991 European Junior 100m title)

'I was expected to win it, and anyone who goes into something expecting to win it always has it on their shoulders. It really gets to me'

RALPH METCALFE (given second in the 1932 Olympic 100m dead-heat under then current rules relating to the torso over the line)

'I only lost the race because I had a bigger fanny'

LEROY BURRELL (on Santa Monica Track Club's success in sprinting)

'The foundation is our training. We train to run fast. We understand the principles of running fast, mechanics of running fast. We have a fast mentality'

LEROY BURRELL (on quality of the sprinters in SMTC)

'When you join Santa Monica you check your ego at the door'

'Relays allow us to compete with one another instead of against one another. I'd hate to line up every weekend against my team-mates'

> **JERRY MAY** (chairman of the US Olympic Sports Psychology Committee)
>
> *'ANGER IS A VASTLY OVER-RATED ASSET. IT LEADS TO INCONSISTENT RESULTS. ANGER CAN TIGHTEN MUSCLES AND INCREASE THE RISK OF INJURY. IT IS ANALOGOUS WITH SEX. TO RESPOND OPTIMALLY, YOU MUST BE EXCITED BUT RELAXED'*

ALF WILKINS (coach and long-time fan – on women's 200m line-up at Crystal Palace, July 1992)

'That's the trouble with female British sprinters. While the foreigners are athletic-looking, ours are short and stout'

(The British runners were Sallyanne Short and Jenny Stoute)

PERCY CERUTTY (Australian coach, guru and, some would say, nut)

*Ready,
Steady,
Go Dean!*

'It can be said right here and now, and without any ambiguity, that the attitudes of some sprinters can never be a fine guide to the states, needs or actions of the middle-distance athlete. Sprinters – usually well-fed, under-exercised by exhaustion standards, and over-adulated by their easier-earned performances – can never be a standard for behaviour'

EVERYTHING'S BETTER IN TEXAS The State of Texas has always produced a good number of top-class sprinters. One of them in the early 1950s was Dean Smith, who gained a gold medal in the sprint relay at the 1952 Olympics in Helsinki. He was particularly known for his fast starting, often questioned by those outside his home environment. In fact a story circulated that at Texas athletic

meets the starter began races with the following variant of the official rules: 'Get to your marks, Get Set, Go Dean,' and then the gun was fired. Smith later became a respected stunt man in Hollywood.

ALL YOU NEED IS . . . American sprint relay teams have never been noted for the slickness of baton-changing which has been evident in the best European teams. Usually this is due to the difficulty of getting team members together from all over a vast country. Also it should be borne in mind that until fairly recently the United States, unlike other countries, rarely competed as a national entity other than in the Olympic Games. Despite this obvious handicap their relay teams have been pre-eminent at the Olympics and in world record lists because of the sheer speed of the four individuals selected. There are two well-known examples of other countries' reactions to this.

In the 1936 Olympic final, the US baton-changing was not very noteworthy but with the likes of Owens, Metcalfe, Draper and Wykoff in the team, it didn't really matter. However, the Germans were certain that their superior technique would triumph. When the Americans' new world record was announced, one of the German team is reported to have commented, 'Suppose you knew how to change the baton?' A grinning Metcalfe retorted, 'Suppose you knew how to run?'

At the Tokyo Olympics in 1964, even the basic speed of the first three runners of the US sprint relay team could not overcome their poor baton-passing technique, and they were way down until Bob Hayes put in a fantastic anchor leg run to clinch the gold medal and break the

world record. A disgruntled French runner muttered to one of them that 'All you had was Hayes', to which the ecstatic American, Paul Drayton, replied, 'Man, that's all we need.'

ANOTHER TIME, ANOTHER PLACE Norris McWhirter tells the story that in 1954 he gave a lift in a taxi to the seven-time winner of the AAA sprint double, McDonald Bailey. After the runner had been dropped off the taxi driver turned and enquired if it had indeed been him. On having his sighting confirmed, the old driver chuckled and gave the opinion that Bailey was 'going to have a job beating this new fella, Gordon Pirie.'

T'WAS EVER THUS When Australian Hector 'Hec' Hogan apparently equalled the world 100m record (10.2) at Sydney in March 1954, he did it in a specially framed handicap race, just an hour

WE HAVE SEEN BETTER DAYS
(Timon of Athens)

One game that dedicated athletics statisticians play is to find different ways to compile their facts. Though of no practical use whatsoever, the following compilation might be of some interest to those with a chronological frame of mind. It consists of the fastest 100m times for the days of the week:

Day	Time	Athlete	Date
Monday	9.95	Jim Hines (USA)	14 Oct 68
Tuesday	9.96	Mel Lattany (USA)	5 May 84
Wednesday	9.93	Carl Lewis (USA)	17 Aug 88
Thursday	9.98	Silvio Leonard (CUB)	11 Aug 77
Friday	9.90	Leroy Burrell (USA)	14 Jun 91
Saturday	9.92	Carl Lewis (USA)	24 Sep 88
Sunday	9.86	Carl Lewis (USA)	25 Aug 91

after legally equalling the 100 yards mark (9.3). There were both men and women placed ahead of him and it has been suggested that he didn't clock an even faster time as he slackened off having 'caught the girls'.

DUCKING AND DIVING In the earlier days of sprinting there were a number of athletes who had very distinctive finishes to their races. In particular the winners of the Olympic 100m in 1920 and 1924 were particularly idiosyncratic. The first, the American Charlie Paddock, used to gather himself and literally leap at the finishing line, often lifting the tape off the chests of his rivals. His successor at the Games, Britain's Harold Abrahams, had a characteristic violent dip at the tape which, as he was a tall man, undoubtedly gained him vital inches.

AN EXACT SCIENCE The great American sprinter of the 1930s, Jesse Owens, was asked what the difference was between the 9.4 100 yards he had run as a high school boy and the 9.4 he ran later as a college student. His answer was a revealing 'About six yards'.

HEY, GOOD-LOOKING British 100m Olympic champion Linford Christie was in 1991 named as the sexiest sportsman in the UK by Brut, the manufacturer of men's toiletries. As well as his sprinting, Linford is also well-known for his skin-tight running gear and as the magazine *Athletics Today* pointed out, it's lucky he can run faster than anyone else in the country.

A RELAY RELIABLE One of the top sprinters of the 1920s and 1930s was Frank Wykoff of the United States. Although he won two US titles, three NCAA championships and ran the first officially accepted 9.4 for 100 yards, he was overshadowed in his individual performances by a host of superb sprinters of the era including Paddock, Tolan, Owens, Peacock and Metcalfe. However, in the relay he gained a niche all of his own as the only man to win three consecutive Olympic sprint relay gold medals, 1928–36. Also, they were all world record-breaking teams.

UP IN THE AIR Probably the first ever altitude-assisted record was the 9.6 for 100 yards by Cyril Coaffee of Canada, set at Calgary in August 1922. This performance, equalling the existing world mark held by three US sprinters, was achieved at an altitude of 1045m (*3436ft*) – a fact which aroused no comment at the time.

OH DARN! On at least two occasions virtually sure-thing Olympic sprint relay gold medals have been lost by runners dropping the baton, both times in women's races. The first occasion was at the Berlin Olympics in 1936. The favourite German team had set a world record of 46.4 in their heat and were leading in the final by about eight metres as they came to the last change-over, from Marie Dollinger to Ilse Dorffeldt. Perhaps ruffled by the cheers of a packed stadium and the presence of Hitler, they fumbled and dropped the baton, allowing the American team to win in 46.9.

There was a happy postscript to this episode at the 1960 Games.

Dollinger's daughter Brunhilde Hendrix was running, also in third position, on the German relay team. One can imagine her watching mother's agonising thoughts as Hendrix came to the change. She passed safely and the German team gained the silver medal.

In 1952 at Helsinki, the Australian 4 × 100m women's team had set a world record in the heat of 46.1. In the final they were leading as they approached the last change-over, from the delightfully named Winsome Cripps to Marjorie Jackson. Jackson had won both the 100m and 200m titles easily, setting world marks in both events, and once she had the baton secure the outcome was assured. However, although the pass was made, as Jackson swung her arm the baton hit Cripp's knee and was knocked out of her hand. As it fell to the track Jackson stopped, picked it up and made off in pursuit, but it was too late. The Americans narrowly beat the Germans, both setting new world figures of 45.9, with Australia in fifth place.

This also had a happy postscript in that one of the 1952 team, Shirley Strickland, who had gained a silver in the relay in 1948, finally won her relay gold in 1956 to add to the other two gold, one silver and three bronze medals she had won in three Games.

HE MOVES IN A MYSTERIOUS WAY James Carlton, three-time Australian 100y/220y champion, ran 220 yards round a bend at Sydney Cricket Ground in January 1932 in a world record time of 20.6 (the three official timekeepers actually all had 20.5). This equalled the time set by an American over a straightaway some years before, but was 0.6

seconds faster than the official turn mark. In the absence of a wind gauge, the referee, who could not believe the time even though Carlton had won by 8 yards from a class sprinter, ruled that it was wind-assisted, although many eye-witnesses reported that there was little or no wind at the time. Nevertheless, the Australian was hailed as a gold medal hope at the Olympic Games in Los Angeles later in the year. However, soon after his 'record' run Carlton retired, at the age of 24, and went into the priesthood. The Olympic title was won by America's Eddie Tolan in 21.2.

JUST A PERFECT FRIENDSHIP
According to Mike Takaha, a coach who works with both Leroy Burrell and Carl Lewis, there are two reasons for their infrequent match-ups. First, the less they race each other the more lucrative their showdowns become. Second, as they work together in practice it would create a strain, as 'you have to have an animosity, not hate but disdain, for opponents.'

ALL ANIMALS ARE EQUAL BUT SOME ARE MORE EQUAL THAN OTHERS (*George Orwell***)**
At the 1988 Olympic Games in Seoul split times were taken in the 100m finals which indicated that Carl Lewis reached a peak speed of 43.37kmh (*26.95mph*) while the women's champion Florence Griffith-Joyner attained 39.56kmh (*24.58mph*). Compared to other members of the animal kingdom these speeds are not very impressive.

The fastest of all land animals is the cheetah with a top speed of about 100kmh (*62mph*) – considerably higher speeds have been claimed but are dismissed by

'Burrell, you're outta here; go try track and field'

most zoologists. Fish have been recorded at speeds in excess of 100kmh, but it is the birds who would win any animal Olympics gold medals. The fastest living creature is thought to be the peregrine falcon which has been clocked at a velocity of 350kmh (*217mph*) while swooping. A number of other birds exceed 105kmh (*65mph*) in level flight.

SPECIAL SKILL After he broke the world 100m record with 9.90 in June 1991, Leroy Burrell said that he probably owed it all to his baseball coach in high school. Apparently the coach told him that he couldn't hit anything, and he couldn't catch anything, but that 'you sure can run bases'. So reluctantly, he tried out for the track team. However, Burrell feels that if he had had any semblance of skill in baseball he would not be in athletics now.

A LEG UP Harry Hillman and Lawson Robertson were two American athletic coaches who, in harness as it were, have an unusual claim to fame. In April 1909 they got together at Brooklyn, New York and recorded a time of 11.0 in a 100 yards three-legged race. That time has never been bettered. As athletes they not surprisingly had excellent credentials. Hillman won three gold medals at the 1904 Olympic Games and later was coach at Dartmouth College for 35 years. Robertson, an American citizen but born in Aberdeen, Scotland, was second in the US 220 yards championship in 1904, the University of Pennsylvania coach for 31 years, and a US Olympic coach at four Games.

HE STOOPS TO CONQUER
There is much confusion about the origins of the crouch start in sprinting. Credit has usually gone to Charles Sherrill, who won the US 100 yards championship in 1887, and his coach Mike Murphy. Sherrill is said to have been seen 'starting on all fours' in 1888 while at Yale University, for whom he won seven inter-collegiate titles. In later life, as General Sherrill and a diplomat, he was named as US

Ambassador to Turkey.

In England, claims have been made for TL Nicholas who apparently used the technique at about the same time, but it is more likely that Bobby McDonald, a New Zealand Maori, was the innovator in 1884.

Of even greater significance was the invention of starting blocks in 1927 by the American coaches George Bresnahan and William Tuttle. However, though used in championships in America the blocks were not allowed for record purposes by the IAAF for many years, and were not used at the Olympic Games until 1952.

MISSING THE POINT
Researchers claim that the first sprinter to use spiked shoes in the United States was William Curtis in 1868, but it is thought that they were previously used in Great Britain, probably by professional runners.

I'M RUNNING BACKWARDS FOR CHRISTMAS *The Guinness Book of Records* records that the fastest time recorded for running the 100m backwards is 13.6 (100 yards in 12.7) by Ferdie Adoboe of Ghana, in America in July 1991. A previous holder of the 100 yards 'record' was the legendary tap dancer Bill 'Bojangles' Robinson, early in the century.

AND MILES TO GO
BEFORE I SLEEP

(Robert Frost)

NEW YORK HERALD TRIBUNE (7 May 1954)

'Let the Aga Khan take what satisfaction he may from his Epsom Derby winners. Let Ben Hogan have the British Open title and welcome. England has the four-minute mile!'

NORRIS McWHIRTER (announcer at Oxford on 6 May 1954)

'Ladies and Gentlemen, here is the result of event number nine, the one mile. First, number 41, RG Bannister of the Amateur Athletic Association and formerly of Exeter and Merton Colleges, with a time which is a new meeting and track record, and which subject to ratification will be a new English Native, British National, British All-Comers', European, British Empire and World's record. The time is Three . . .'

(The rest of the announcement was drowned by the roar of the crowd)

SEBASTIAN COE (twice Olympic 1500m champion – on his coach, Peter Coe)

'The partnership with my father has worked because I like the guy. I would even like him if he were not my father. He can be a bit brutal, certainly, but he has been right so often. When I was only 13 he drew up a projection of progress for me with an optimum 1500m time of 3:30.0, and that at a time when I had achieved only 4:31.8 and the world record was 3:35.6'

(Coe eventually ran 3:29.77 in 1986)

JOHN WALKER (1976 Olympic 1500m champion and first sub-3:50.0 miler)

'Naturally, you have to be born with some sort of talent, whether it is playing a piano, running or whatever. I think I was very lucky to have this because my father was a runner and I have virtually inherited it from him. But I still had to work on it and it has not been easy, though maybe I have had it a little easier than some people'

NOUREDDINE MORCELI (1991 World 1500m champion – on altitude training)

'I don't think it matters. I remember in 1990 that I never went to altitude and I still ran 3:32.0. If you train hard you will be the best'

ROGER BANNISTER (reflecting on the first sub-4 minute mile)

'I think the four-minute mile has been over-rated. After all it's only a time – the essence of athletics is racing against opponents rather than against the clock'

PETER ELLIOTT (1990 Commonwealth 1500m champion)

'When I finish running I won't sit around at home. I'll go out and find a job. Most athletes reach the end of their careers and suddenly they've got nothing left and they feel the world owes them a job. They don't think that when they stop running someone else will come up, but that's how it is'

STEVE CRAM (former World, European and Commonwealth 1500m champion, in 1991)

'There are times when one athlete seems supreme in their event. At 1500m it was Ovett for a while, then Coe, then me. It could have been Peter (Elliott) last year, but he was injured. At the moment it's Morceli. It might last a year, it might last for five. But it doesn't last for ever'

SEBASTIAN COE (commenting on Steve Ovett in a TV programme about them both)

'I find no difficulty in saying that he is the greatest runner I ever competed against, probably the most complete athlete I knew'

STEVE OVETT (commenting on Sebastian Coe in a TV programme about them both)

'Seb always, in my mind, has been one of the greatest athletes we've ever seen. I was always aware of that fact. A far better athlete than I am. A far better natural talent than I ever was'

PETER COE (in 1972 to son Seb, aged 14)

'I don't want this to come as a major surprise to you but you will be going

> **ABEL KIVIAT** (*1912 Olympic 1500m silver medallist – interviewed by the* New York Times *aged 99, he said he was looking for a wife*)
>
> *'SHE DOES NOT HAVE TO HAVE TEETH, SHE JUST HAS TO HAVE A DRIVER'S LICENCE'*

to the Olympic Games in 1980, and I've seen a lot of athletes wilt under that kind of pressure, and I want you to get used to it now'

JOHN LANDY (reaction to plans for a statue commemorating the moment he was passed by Bannister in the 1954 Commonwealth Games mile)

'I'll be remembered as the man who looked over his shoulder and lost the race. I can't complain. Lot's wife looked over her shoulder and was turned into a pillar of salt. I looked over mine and I've been turned into a pillar of bronze'

MARTY LIQUORI (former American miler – on the public perception of the different areas of the sport)

'Running on the track is Carnegie Hall, on the road is rock 'n' roll'

TREADING THE BOARDS One of the more unusual 'tracks' on which athletics has been held was the famous Boardwalk at Atlantic City, New Jersey. In 1953 and 1954 mile races were held over a carefully measured course, with the fastest time achieved being 4:06.3 by the British runner Alex Breckinridge in the latter year.

I'VE ONLY GOT FOUR MINUTES (*catchphrase of Australian comedian Bill Kerr***)** Since Roger Bannister cracked the 'barrier' on 6 May 1954, it has been broken over 3430 times, to the end of 1992. A total of 6707 runners from 43 countries had achieved the feat in 1122 races. The most prolific country has been the United States with 187 athletes, while Great Britain comes next with 134. The greatest number of sub-4 miles by one athlete has been 139 by Steve Scott (USA), with New Zealand's John Walker the runner-up with 129. The greatest number of runners to break 4 minutes in one race is 14 at Koblenz, Germany on 25 August 1982. The race was won by Steve Scott in 3:49.72 and all 14 actually ran sub-3:59.0. On 8 August 1980 13 men ran sub-4 minutes at Berlin, while at Crystal Palace on the same day another 13 achieved it.

The youngest runner to accomplish it was Jim Ryun (USA) in 1964 aged 17 years 37 days, while the oldest was Kenya's Mike Boit in 1987 aged 38 years 227 days.

The first man to be given the time of exactly 4 minutes was Derek Ibbotson (GBR) when he placed fourth in a race at White City in 1958. Given the same time but placed fifth was Mike Blagrove (GBR), who had paced Ibbotson to his world record 3:57.2 the previous year.

LOVE AND MARRIAGE Steve Ovett created a lot of media interest in 1980–81 when after races, which he invariably won, he would gesture in the air the letters, I, L and Y. The press soon discovered that it meant 'I Love You', and was directed at his fiancée Rachel. A year or so later, by which time he had ceased the practice, a TV commentator referred to it thus: 'And there's no "I Love You" message because Steve Ovett married the girl.'

EARS BURNING? There are some fans and officials today who remember with some pleasure a decision made at the 1954 Soviet championships in Kiev. Vladimir Okorokov finished first in the 1500m in 3:54.6 (some 5 seconds slower than in his heat) but was denied the title and the winner's prize. An official announcement noted, 'Instead of running to the best of his possibilities, he let others set the pace and just forged ahead in the last few metres to win a cheap victory.'

YOU DID WHAT? In the euphoria of the world record mile on 6 May 1954, not many people took much notice of Oxford hurdler Paul Vine's claim to have crossed the finish line ahead of Roger Bannister. In the strictly legal sense (and he was the son of a well-known magistrate) Vine was correct as he had been last in the race preceding the mile.

A couple of years after he had become the world's first sub-4 minute miler, and won the European and Commonwealth titles, Roger Bannister met up with a former school acquaintance. Rather hesitantly the friend said that he thought he had heard from another friend that Bannister had taken up running. 'You know,' he said, 'sometimes I also feel like taking some exercise, but I just lie down and rest until the feeling has passed.'

GENTLEMAN RUNNER In the 1956 Australian mile championship there was a remarkable occurrence, which may have been the greatest performance in the fine career of former world record holder John

Landy. With about 600 yards to go, the national junior record holder Ron Clarke fell. Landy was just able to scramble over him and in so doing inadvertently spiked Clarke's arm. He ran on a few yards, pulled onto the grass and came back to Clarke to see if he was okay. The youngster remonstrated with him to get going and Landy turned to see the rest of the field some 50 yards on. Realising that Clarke was not too badly hurt, the world record holder set off after the others, having lost an estimated 5–6 seconds. He caught up and won the race in 4:04.2. Clarke carried the torch into the Olympic stadium in Melbourne later that year and became one of the all-time greats of distance runnning.

TO LIVE BACKWARDS FROM THE FRONT As a sprinter in my youth who found the furlong a long way, sadly missing feeding stations around the bend, the classic mile distance was for this author an unattainable Holy Grail. I once ran a 1500m in a pentathlon, under great pressure from my peers, clocking outside 7 minutes (mile equivalent about 7½min) which gave me no points on the then-current tables. Thus one of the most amazing performances, to me, was that of Donald Davis (USA) in 1983 when he ran the mile *backwards* in 6:07.1.

VERSATILITY Most great middle-distance runners have an outstanding range, able to achieve world-class performances over a number of distances, but Britain has produced more than its fair share of such men. Two outstanding ones have been Sydney Wooderson and Steve Ovett. Before World War II,

Wooderson set world record marks over 880y and 1 mile, and won the 1938 European 1500m title. After the war, which undoubtedly robbed him of further great achievements, he won the 1946 European 5000m crown and in 1948 won the English National Cross-Country championship over a distance of 9 miles (*14.5km*).

Ovett, having started his career with a national schools title at 400m, set world marks at 1500m, 1 mile and 2 miles, and more unusually won international titles at 800m (1980 Olympic Games), 1500m (1978 European) and 5000m (1986 Commonwealth Games).

O SOLE MIO The only man to win both the Olympic and European Championship 1500m titles was Luigi Beccali of Italy in 1932 and 1934 respectively. In 1933 he twice set world marks for the distance, and gained bronze medals in the 1936 Olympics and 1938 Europeans.

CLASS WILL TELL In the 1989 AAA 1500m final the field was bunching as they approached the bell after a fairly slow early pace. The 1987 champion Steve Crabb suddenly stumbled and fell, causing Seb Coe to cut stride and hurdle over him – losing some 10 or 15 metres, straining his left hamstring and dropping back to eighth place in the process. Despite all this, Coe went after the field like a sprinter and covering the last lap in 51.8, of which the last 200m was 25.4, he caught everyone and won the race in 3:41.38. Remarkably, just short of his 33rd birthday, it was the first senior AAA 1500m title for the double Olympic champion.

RULE BRITANNIA . . .

One of the most remarkable periods of domination of an event, or events, occurred from 1977 to 1988. During that time British middle-distance runners established a hold on the major titles at 800m and 1500m that had never been matched before. Listed below is the roll of honour:

		Gold	Silver	Bronze
Olympic Games:				
1980	800m	Ovett	Coe	
1980	1500m	Coe		Ovett
1984	800m		Coe	
1984	1500m	Coe	Cram	
1988	1500m		Elliott	
European Championships:				
1978	800m		Ovett	Coe
1978	1500m	Ovett		Moorcroft
1982	800m		Coe	
1982	1500m	Cram		
1986	800m	Coe	McKean	Cram
1986	1500m	Cram	Coe	
Commonwealth Games:				
1978	1500m	Moorcroft	Robson	
1982	800m		McGeorge	
1982	1500m	Cram		
1986	800m	Cram	McKean	Elliott
1986	1500m	Cram	Gladwin	
European Indoor Championships:				
1977	800m	Coe		
1979	1500m			Robson
1983	800m		Elliott	
1984	800m			Norgate
1985	800m	Harrison		
1988	800m	Sharpe		
World Indoor Championships:				
1985	800m			Billy
European Cup:				
1979	800m	Coe		
1981	800m	Coe		
1981	1500m			Cram
1983	800m			Elliott
1983	1500m	Cram		
1985	800m	McKean		
1985	1500m	Cram		
1987	800m	McKean		
1987	1500m			Cram
World Cup:				
1981	800m	Coe		
1981	1500m	Ovett		

... BRITANNIA RULES THE LANES

In addition to the above medals British middle-distance runners were rewriting the world record books with the following performances:

800m:
 1:42.33 ....Sebastian Coe ....July 1989
 1:41.73 ....Sebastian Coe ....June 1981 (*still current mark*)

1000m:
 2:13.40 ....Sebastian Coe ....July 1980
 2:12.18 ....Sebastian Coe ....July 1981 (*still current mark*)

1500m:
 3:32.1 ......Sebastian Coe ....August 1979
 3:32.1 ......Steve Ovett ....July 1980
 3:31.36 ....Steve Ovett ....August 1980
 3:30.77 ....Steve Ovett ....September 1983
 3:29.67 ....Steve Cram ....July 1985 (*still European record*)

Mile:
 3:49.0 ......Sebastian Coe ....July 1979
 3:48.8 ......Steve Ovett ....July 1980
 3:48.53 ....Sebastian Coe ....August 1981
 3:48.40 ....Steve Ovett ....August 1981
 3:47.33 ....Sebastian Coe ....August 1981
 3:46.32 ....Steve Cram ....July 1985 (*still current mark*)

2000m:
 4:51.39 ....Steve Cram ....August 1985 (*still European record*)

4 × 800m:
 7:03.89 ....GB Team ....August 1982 (*still current mark*)
 (Peter Elliott, Gary Cook, Steve Cram, Seb Coe)

THEY DON'T MAKE 'EM TOUGH IN THE WEST A month after Roger Bannister ran the first sub-four minute mile at Oxford in May 1954, his great American rival Wes Santee attempted the feat for the umpteenth time. Running at the famous Compton meeting in California he only clocked 4:00.6, albeit breaking the world 1500m mark en route. He and his advisers commented that the weather had been rather too cool at 63 degrees fahrenheit. Seven days later Santee tried again at Los Angeles, and clocked 4:00.7 – although even warmer than the week before, the weather was still reported to have been too cold. At Oxford the weather had been so bad that the attempt was very nearly called off, and the temperature was certainly no better than 50 degrees, possibly worse.

IF YOU CAN'T, YOU CAN'T After placing third in the 1972 Olympic 1500m at Munich, Rod Dixon of New Zealand could only produce a very small sample for the urine test. On his asking whether that would suffice, the German official answered, 'For the gold medal, no; but for the bronze, it will do.'

OH, MY DARLING CLEMENTINE? One of the strangest mile runs occurred in 1991 down a mineshaft in the Eastern Transvaal, South Africa, some 100m underground. The current South African distance running sensation Elana Meyer ran the distance in 4:34.0. According to a report in *Athletics Today* the shaft was apparently very clean, and so well lit that the event was televised.

AND FOR MY NEXT TRICK In 1990 four 'jogglers' ran a mile relay in a record 3:57.38. Each runner continuously juggled three balls throughout their leg, the 'baton' being one of the balls.

Here come the 'jogglers'

TO ERR IS HUMAN Derek Ibbotson broke the world record for 1 mile in July 1957, running 3:57.2 at the White City, London.

Exactly one week before that he had been eliminated from the final of the AAA mile, failing to win his heat. It should be noted, however, that on the following day he had come back to not only win the national 3 mile title but also break the UK record.

JESHURUN WAXED FAT, AND KICKED (*Deuteronomy*) There have been many superlative last laps in mile and 1500m races, but the fastest kick in a world-class race must surely have been that exhibited by Jim Ryun in Dusseldorf in August 1967. The previous month he had set a new world record for the metric distance and on this occasion he was running for the USA against West Germany. His opponents were Bodo Tummler and Harald Norpoth and his teammate was Jim Grelle – all three of them top-class athletes in their own right.

The early pace was fairly slow and Ryun and the Germans passed the bell in 2:47.2. At 1200m the American changed gear and went, covering that last 300m in a staggering 36.2 seconds (about 48.3 pace for 400m). The winning time of 3:38.2 was only beaten by Ryun himself and Keino that year.

SHORT AND SWEET In the first issue (March 1952) of their excellent magazine *Athletics World*, the McWhirter twins caused quite a stir when they revealed that the United States Standard Mile was actually 3/8th of an inch shorter than the UK Statute Mile. The implication of all those 'phoney' American mile times was horrendous. However, to put the whole thing into perspective, Norris worked out that it would make a difference of only 0.86082 of a mile in the distance from Earth to the Moon.

THE MOUNTAINS LOOK ON MARATHON

(Lord Byron)

TOSHIHIKO SEKO (1986 London marathon champion – known for his ascetic attitude to training and running)

'The marathon is my only girlfriend'

JERRY COYLE (American runner)

'I suppose the marathon is like a wedding day. You plan for it, wait for it, and you want to remember every little detail about it. And then it's over so quickly'

ANONYMOUS

'Some people say that being involved in running a marathon is the same as the commitment shown by any top athlete. They are not the same. Think of it like ham and eggs. The chicken is involved, but the pig is committed'

KITEI SON (aka Sohn Kee-Chung) (1936 Olympic marathon champion)

'The human body can do just so much – then the heart and spirit must take over'

HUGH JONES (1982 London marathon champion, writing in 1992)

'Marathon runners circle the Earth like carrion crows on the lookout for pickings from the fast lane'

HIROMI TANIGUCHI (1991 World marathon champion, on why he took up the marathon)

'As a child I was not allowed to drink juice. When I was a middle-school student I watched a marathon race and saw the runners drinking a liquid, which I thought was juice. So I thought a marathon might be tough – but I could drink juice while I was running'

DON KARDONG (American marathon runner – on receiving money for running)

'We don't lose respect for a professional athlete because he gets money for his sport. We lose respect for him if, and only if, he ceases to love his profession'

MICHAEL BLAND (Reader's letter to *Athletics Weekly* in April 1992)

'We are advised to stop training if we experience a number of symptoms, including general fatigue, loss of motivation, poor sleep, general depression and loss of sex drive. I'm like that every morning. Should I give up training for good?'

PAUL DAVIES-HALE (One of Britain's selections for Barcelona in 1992)

'It's going to be a strange experience running a marathon for nothing. We must be mad!'

ANDREA WALLACE (British distance star on her 1992 London marathon run)

'All of a sudden it was like being hit by a brick wall. My legs weren't working properly any more, although my breathing was superb. I just couldn't lift my legs. It's unbelievable how I could feel so brilliant and then lose it in the last three miles, but that's what happens in a marathon'

ALLISTER HUTTON (After winning 1990 London marathon)

'I woke up the next morning feeling as though I had been run over by a bus, and it took me nearly a month before I could start running freely again'

CHRIS BRASHER (Writing in the *Observer*, after competing in 1979 New York marathon)

'To believe this story you must believe that the human race can be one joyous family, working together, laughing together, achieving the impossible. Last Sunday, in one of the most violent, trouble-stricken cities in the world, 11 532 men and women from over 40 countries in the world, assisted by over a million black, white, and yellow people, laughed, cheered and suffered during the greatest folk festival the world has seen'

SALVADOR GARCIA (Mexican winner of the 1991 New York marathon)

'Because of the topography and altitude, Mexicans are the strongest runners, or should be. If we are more disciplined, we will achieve that. We need to attack. We can't be intimidated by the Kenyans'

JEROME DRAYTON (Canadian winner of 1977 Boston marathon)

'To describe the agony of the marathon to somebody who's never run it is like trying to explain colour to a person who was born blind'

PAUL DAVIES-HALE (After finishing 4th in the 1991 Carpi race in 2hr11:57)

'I was sprinting at the finish, which you shouldn't really be doing in the marathon. You should be staggering in'

ANDREA WALLACE (On hitting the mythical 'wall' in her second marathon, London 1992)

'We weren't really racing until 20[miles]. I felt I was really good at this stage. One minute I was thinking I could win because it was so easy, the next I was trying to run to get third position'

(She did)

SALLY EASTALL (After improving by over 5 minutes to win the 1991 Sacramento marathon with 2hr29:29 and clinch Olympic selection)

'It was a shock to me as well. I wasn't really planning to run that fast. My coach wanted me to run it steadily to be sure of getting the qualifying time (2hr35:00). But I just felt good, went out too fast and managed to keep it going'

TO BE THE BEST Who is the best marathon runner of all time? There is probably no definitive answer to the question, but one can suggest a few athletes who must be in the reckoning for such an accolade. The main criterion for such a selection must surely be a runner's performances in major championship races. On this basis, Portugal's Rosa Mota comes out top. Since switching to the marathon in 1982 she has won three European titles, one Olympic gold (plus a bronze) and one World title (plus a fourth place). In addition she has won the London, Chicago, Tokyo, Boston and Osaka races at least once.

No man can match the above series of performances, but there is a complication when trying to compare the main contenders for the male crown. That is the situation confronting non-European runners, who cannot always be assessed on the basis of the same races as Mota. For example, Abebe Bikila of Ethiopia won two Olympic races (1960–64) which must rank him very high in any list. Injury forced him out of the 1968 Games and sadly he was paralysed in a car accident the following year. He did not have the opportunity to compete in the world championships as they were not instituted until 1983. Also, of course, he was ineligible for the European title.

Perhaps a slightly higher rating should be assigned to Waldemar Cierpinski who won two Olympic gold medals for the GDR (1976–80). In addition to these he also gained a third place in the 1983 World title race and placed 4th and 6th in the European championships. Another who has a fine record in championship races is Karel Lismont of Belgium. He won the 1971 European title, adding bronzes in the 1978 and 1982 races; gained an Olympic silver (1972) and bronze (1976) plus a 9th place in 1980; and placed 9th in the 1983 World championship.

Worthy of honourable mention are Frank Shorter (USA), winner of gold (1972) and silver (1976) Olympic medals, plus four wins in the prestigious Fukuoka race; Gelindo Bordin of Italy who has won two European golds (1986–90), the 1988 Olympic title, and placed third (1983) and eighth (1991) in World championship races; and Rob de Castella of Australia, the winner of the first World title in 1983, twice Commonwealth champion (1982–86), placed 10th, 5th and 8th in three Olympic races (1980–88) and a winner at Fukuoka and Boston.

YOU'VE BEEN TOLD The official booklet on the Boston marathon has some excellent advice that is not always followed by competitors: 'The start is downhill and easy, but soon there is an uphill, so watch out that early enthusiasm to maintain speed does not force you into oxygen debt. . . . Then there are some little hills here and you could be tempted to charge up them – watch out, and don't.'

ON THE JOB TRAINING The first African runner to win an Olympic gold medal was Mohamed Boughera El Ouafi, an Algerian running for France. In 1928 at Amsterdam he won the marathon, having placed seventh four years earlier. Off the sports field he had been a French Army dispatch runner.

ANYTHING YOU CAN DO As Abebe Bikila of Ethiopia crossed the finish line at Tokyo in 1964, having successfully defended his

Olympic title, he shrugged off the blanket offered to all the finishers and went into a bending and stretching routine which brought gasps and laughter from the watching thousands. Old-timers among them were reminded of an Italian, Valerio Arri, who finished in third place at Antwerp in 1920 and celebrated by doing cartwheels as he crossed the line.

EVER-PRESENT One of the truly great marathon runners must be John Adelbert Kelley of the United States. Not because he won the US championship on two occasions, nor because he won the famed Boston race twice. More uniquely, when he ran in the 1992 edition of that Boston marathon it was the 61st time he had participated. In 1991, at the age of 83, he clocked 5hr42:54, the 57th time he had completed the course since 1928. Asked to explain his running longevity, he said, 'If I don't run for a few days I feel as if something has been stolen from me.' There are plans to set up a 4.26m (*14ft*) sculpture of him at about the 19.2 mile (*31km*) mark.

THE FICKLE FINGER OF FATE
When Ethiopia's Abebe Bikila won his second Olympic marathon title in 1964 at Tokyo, a thrilling duel was going on behind him between Japan's Kokichi Tsuburaya and Britain's Basil Heatley. While Bikila, who had finished over 4 minutes ahead, did his relaxing exercises on the infield, Tsuburaya entered the stadium with Heatley close behind him. As they went into the final bend the Briton sprinted past the exhausted Japanese runner to take the silver medal. Although Tsuburaya's was the only athletics medal won by

Japan in Tokyo, and their first since 1936, the humiliation of being passed in front of 75 000 of his own people rankled. In January 1968, under great pressure to restore his honour at Mexico City and bedevilled by injuries, he took his own life.

Yet another tragedy befell one of the 1964 runners. This time it was the winner, Abebe Bikila. Attempting to win his third title at Mexico City, he had to retire with a leg injury. In 1969, while driving the car given to him by a grateful government after his Tokyo victory, he crashed, suffering serious spinal injuries which left him paralysed below the waist. He spent the rest of his life in a wheelchair, dying of a brain haemorrhage in 1973 when only 41 years old.

> **ANONYMOUS** (*discussing a club runner*)
> 'HE'S SO SLOW YOU COULD TIME HIM WITH A SUNDIAL'

FIFTY MILLION FRENCHMEN CAN'T BE WRONG – CAN THEY? The first gold medal for France in Olympic athletics was won by Michel Theato in the 1900 marathon in Paris. The race was run in incredible heat with the temperature reaching 39 degrees centigrade (102°F) and the winner finished 4½ minutes ahead of the second man, also from France. However, a leading French researcher has discovered that Theato, a baker's delivery boy, was not a Frenchman at all – he was actually born in Luxembourg. It is understood that no changes will be made to the unofficial medal tables despite this revelation.

At the next Games in St Louis in 1904 it was only a little cooler, at 32 degrees centigrade (90°F). With

'How come he doesn't know the Star-Spangled Banner?'

very few foreigners at these Games because of the travelling distance involved, it was initially reported that the first three places went to Americans. Over 70 years later an American Olympic expert, Bill Mallon, discovered that the silver medallist was in fact a Frenchman. By profession a strikebreaker, Albert Coray had gone to work in Chicago the previous year and had been entered by his American club. Since he was in no way a US citizen the medal tables have been amended and France has gained another medal. Of even more interest is the fact that France was not officially at these Games and so the emergence of Coray's real nationality also amends the number of countries which took part in St Louis from 12 to 13. The actual winner in 1904 was Thomas Hicks, who although born in Birmingham, England, had become an American citizen.

THE TWILIGHT ZONE Much has been written and spoken over the years about 'unknowns' in the sport, but only rarely has the epithet been correctly and honestly applied. Without doubt one such case was Gidemas Shahanga of Tanzania at the 1978 Commonwealth Games in Edmonton, Canada. Prior to the race the media experts and most of his own team knew nothing about him whatsoever. Not even his age, let alone any performances, and as the runners approached the stadium, with Shahanga rapidly closing the gap on the leader, panic broke out. The author, working for BBC TV, rushed to the computer in the Press room, but there was no entry against the African runner's name.

As I ran back to the commentary box, I inadvertently bumped into two men who by incredible chance happened to be part of the Tanzanian management. Gasping out my request, I learned that they too knew nothing – until one of them remembered that Shahanga had finished 7th in that year's African championships after stopping to take off his brand-new running shoes. They also guessed, pretty accurately it turned out, at his age and I fell into the box with just enough breath left to pass on these few details to the commentators, just as Shahanga entered the stadium to take the title. His time was well over 10 minutes faster than he had ever run before, and he heralded a wave of great African marathon runners.

IDEOLOGY TO THE FORE
When marathon runner Ivan Filin of the Soviet Union led into the stadium in the 1954 European championships at Berne, Switzerland, he was confused by officials and (perhaps due to his upbringing) turned left in error. By the time he had been corrected two others had gone the correct way, to the right, and he was only able to finish in third place. Though the result had to stand, Filin was later presented with a special gold medal.

STIMULATE THE PHAGOCYTES (*From The Doctor's Dilemma by GB Shaw*)
The first known use of stimulants in 'amateur' sport was the reported supply of strychnine given to the winner of the 1904 Olympic marathon, Thomas Hicks, by his attendants during the race. However, it is known that the substance was used widely by 19th century professionals, particularly during endurance racing.

WHAT MIGHT HAVE BEEN The great Finnish runner Paavo Nurmi hoped to close his fantastic career by running in the Olympic marathon of 1932, in an effort to add to his haul of 9 gold and 3 silver medals from the previous three Games. Unfortunately he fell foul of amateur laws for accepting excessive expenses on an exhibition tour and was banned almost at the last moment. In fact he appeared in a Finnish team handbook for the Games, which indicated that he had run a 40.2km race in June in a very fast 2hr23min. This indicates that he could have run the full distance (42.195km) in under 2½ hours. Since the eventual winner, Zabala of Argentina, clocked 2hr31:36 and the Finn Armas Toivonen was only 36 seconds behind in third place, it seems more than likely that Nurmi would have gained a medal, and probably it would have been gold.

THIS MUST BE THE PLACE The AAA championships in 1946 were not particularly well organised and the leading marathon runners came into the White City stadium earlier than planned for. Unfortunately the 2 mile steeplechase was still being contested and Squire Yarrow and Donald McNab Robertson must have wondered what madhouse they had stumbled into as they had to weave in and out of steeplechasers and steeplechase barriers. Despite or perhaps because of these problems they staged one of the closest finishes ever seen in a marathon, with Yarrow taking the title from Robertson by 0.2 second.

SINGLE-MINDED Ron Hill, the British winner of the 1969 European, 1970 Commonwealth and 1970 Boston marathons, had completed 201 168km (*125 000 miles*) of running by May 1992. Now 53, he notes that they are all listed in his training log, which he began in September 1956, and emphasises that he has not missed a single day's running since December 1964 – 10 000 consecutive training days. He has also competed in a record 53 countries.

BROTHER MINE Thomas Robert Naali of Tanzania was a 2hr18min marathon runner who was in the 1992 London marathon to make the pace for the 'better' runners. His name was respected, but only because his elder brother Simon was considered world class and had placed third in the 1990 Commonwealth Games. Thomas and another younger brother Francis, also a runner, lived in Simon's shadow. The instructions to Thomas were concise: to take out a good pace for halfway and then do what he liked, drop out or run at his own pace. He did his job well, running forcibly and soon there were only two others with him. After halfway he continued in place, sometimes leading, sometimes dropping to third, but going well. With a mile or two to go it seemed that he might win, but in the end it proved too much for him. Nevertheless, the 'pacemaker' had placed third and clocked 2hr10:08, which in fact was faster than brother Simon had ever run. Francis clocked 2hr36:13. Apparently there is a fourth brother Agebit, only 16 at the moment, who they think will be far better than any of them.

The fastest brothers, in fact twins, of all time were Takeshi and Shigeru Soh of Japan, who clocked 2hr08:55 (1983) and 2hr09:06 (1978) respectively.

STAR OF AFRICA What may be the most successful winning streak in marathon history was that by the great Ethiopian runner Abebe Bikila between 1960 and 1966, when he came first in 12 of 13 races which included two Olympic titles.

UNDER-TRAINED A British computer controller from Coventry, 29-year-old Steve Edwards, completed his record 87th marathon within a year in the Olympic Stadium at Barcelona on 15 March 1992. In total he ran over 2280 racing miles (*3668km*) including one race held indoors which necessitated covering 212 laps of the 200m track. On 30 occasions he ran marathons back to back, that is two races on consecutive days, often hundreds of miles apart, and at least six of the races were in excess of 50km (*30 miles*). He says that the easiest bit was the running. The main problem was staying fit and healthy for 12 months.

A previous record holder was Jay Helgerson of California who had run a marathon or longer every week for 52 weeks. Asked for the secret of his success he had replied, tongue in cheek, that he didn't train very much between races.

An American, Sy Mah, didn't start running the marathon until 1966 when he was 40, but in the next 22 years he ran a record 524 of them.

Dubious encouragement for track-marathon runners

A Swede, Kjell-Eric Stahl, has run a record 69 times under 2hr20:00 for the distance.

STEPPING OUT It has been calculated that an average runner will take about 1000 steps per mile in a marathon. That means a total of approximately 26 200 steps during a race. It is not difficult to understand the need to wear a well-padded shoe.

WHEN MEN WERE MEN The first man to run the marathon in under 2hr20:00 was Jim Peters of Essex Beagles. In the 1952 AAA race, which was part of the famed Poly marathon that year, he had brought the world best down to within 42.3 seconds of the landmark. The following year was the 40th anniversary of the Poly and he took the opportunity to cut the record to 2hr18:40.2. Six months later in Finland he shaved another few seconds off and then in 1954, again in the Poly race, he brought it down to 2hr17:39.4. It is worth noting that in these races he ran in gym shoes, which had little or no padding underfoot.

ARGY-BARGY With all the current interest in Kenyan runners and their domination of distance running, few people remember the time when another country, from a more unlikely part of the world, seemed to produce champion after champion. That country was Argentina, and from 1932 to 1952 their runners gave nightmares to the world's marathon men. In 1931 Juan Carlos Zabala had beaten the world's best time for 30km on the track, and at Los Angeles the following year he just held on to win his country's first Olympic title in athletics. In Berlin in 1936 he set off far too fast and after leading for over half the race was forced to drop out some 10km from the finish.

Argentina gained its revenge at the next Games in 1948 at London, when a virtual unknown, Delfo Cabrera, in his first marathon race, won the Olympic title. In 1952, second to the amazing Emil Zatopek was Renaldo Gorno, little-known despite his second place to team-mate Cabrera in the 1951 Pan-American championship. Cabrera, the defending Olympic champion, placed a creditable 6th – and thus passed an era. Since then no South American distance runner has gained an Olympic or World Championship medal.

LIFE'S A MERRY-GO-ROUND Four months after being disqualified in the 1908 Olympic marathon, Dorando Pietri of Italy met the Olympic champion Johnny Hayes (USA) again, this time on the Madison Square Garden indoor track for a special race over the marathon distance. As the track measured 160.93m in circumstances they had to run 262 laps. Pietri won in 2hr44:20.4, just under ten minutes faster than his London time had been, with Hayes about 45 seconds behind.

MAN'S BEST FRIEND? In the 1950 Empire Games marathon race the eventual winner, England's Jack Holden, was well ahead with just a couple of miles to go when he was attacked by, of all things, a Great Dane. The dog was possibly attracted by the fact that Holden had discarded his soaking wet shoes after a rainstorm. Jack was more shaken than hurt and went on later in the year to win the European title as well.

Korea's Yun Bok Suh, who was only 1.55m (*5ft 1in*) tall, won the 1947 Boston marathon in world record time despite being bowled over by a boisterous dog on the course. A compatriot of his, Yung-Jo Whang, won the 1991 World Student Games marathon in Sheffield in a new Games record of 2hr12:40. He undoubtedly had some assistance as it was reported that a small dog, belonging to the landlord of a public house en route, ran at the passing runners and snapped viciously at their heels. As a bystander said, 'It must have improved his time no end.'

NO LAUGHING MATTER Fred Lorz of the United States dropped out of the 1904 Olympic marathon after about 10 miles and got a lift in a car to within a few miles of the stadium. As a joke, he claimed afterwards, he then ran into the stadium, was declared the winner, and was about to be awarded the gold medal when his deception was discovered. Initially he was banned for life by the American authorities, but was later reinstated. The real winner Thomas Hicks, a British-born American, arrived some 15 minutes later. Coincidentally, Hicks was a clown by profession. Mentally and physically drained by the experience, Hicks never ran again.

A FRIGHTFUL FIEND DOTH CLOSE BEHIND HIM TREAD (*Samuel Coleridge*) The closest finish in Olympic marathon history occurred in 1920. Hannes Kolehmainen, the first of the famous Flying Finns and a triple gold medallist from the 1912 Games, beat Juri Lossman of Estonia by only 12.8 seconds. As a matter of interest, the distance of the race that year was a unique 42 750 metres, the longest ever. (The current marathon distance is 42.195km.) Since then there have been four occasions on which the gap has been only a few seconds more: 1932 (19 seconds), 1948 (16), 1980 (17) and 1988 (15). In the latter race the bronze medallist was a mere 12 seconds further back.

The biggest margin of victory in the Olympic marathon was in the very first one in 1896. The distance (40km) was somewhat shorter than today, being the distance from the village of Marathon to Athens, but Spiridon Louis beat a fellow-Greek by 7 minutes 13 seconds.

The narrowest winning margin ever recorded in a major title marathon occurred in 1978 at the European Championships when Leonid Moiseyev (URS) beat his countryman Nikolai Penzin by 1.5 seconds. Coincidentally, Moiseyev also came first in an incredibly close finish in the 1979 Moscow marathon in which the first three men were all given the same official time of 2hr13:20, although the automatic timing showed differentials of 0.2 seconds between first and second, and second and third. Even more remarkably, the fourth man was given 2hr13:21 and only six seconds separated the winner from sixth place.

There have been some excessive margins of victory in some minor races, such as 30 minutes 32 seconds in the 1976 Pan-Arab Games marathon. However, even the US championship race has seen a 19min 46sec gap when Buddy Edelen won in 1964, and the 1934 AAA title was won by

Donald McNab Robertson who finished 13min 10sec ahead of the second man.

A CROWD IS NOT COMPANY
(*Old proverb*) The New York Police Department estimated that some 2 million people stood along the route of the New York marathon in 1991. However, an unofficial estimate of the crowd watching the 1982 edition of the race was 2.5–3 million. The New York race is a mixed one, i.e. male and female runners, and the 'record' number of spectators for a women-only marathon was put at 1.5 million at the Osaka marathon in 1981.

TO GIVE THEIR ALL
It is generally acknowledged that Britain's Jim Peters transformed the marathon with a series of record-breaking runs in the 1950s. Despite his failure in the Olympic marathon at Helsinki in 1952, when he was forced out of the race by cramp, he established an enviable record by setting new world standards on four occasions between 1952 and 1954, taking a total of 8 minutes off the previous best. However, he is probably most famous for a race he did not win – the 1954 Empire Games race in Vancouver in August 1954.

In scorching heat he set a very fast pace and entered the stadium some 20 minutes ahead of the next man. However, severe heat exhaustion suddenly got to him and he lost control of his legs and balance. Over the next 300 yards or so he stumbled and fell like a drunken man. His iron will drove him on to what he thought was the finishing line, but it was not the correct line for the marathon finish. Officials, who had been unsure whether to go to his aid,

thereby disqualifying him à la Dorando Pietri at the 1908 Olympics, finally rushed to help him. He was taken to hospital where he did not recover consciousness until the following day. He never ran competitively again. It was noted that, coincidentally, Peters is probably the English equivalent of Pietri.

A scene reminiscent of Vancouver occurred in the Los Angeles Coliseum at the end of the inaugural Olympic women's marathon in 1984. Well after the winner had crossed the line and most of the field had finished, Swiss runner Gaby Andersen-Scheiss, who actually lived in Idaho, staggered into the stadium. Suffering from serious heat exhaustion she looked somewhat like a ragged doll, with one arm hanging limp and one leg apparently very stiff. With the crowd first cheering her on, and then calling for officials to stop her, she circled the track, sometimes stopping, other times pitifully staggering along, until finally she reached the finish line and collapsed. As medical staff took her away it was noted that she had finished in 37th place. Happily she recovered quite quickly and was back running within a couple of weeks.

IT'S ALL GREEK TO ME
The modern marathon race is based on a story from antiquity which may or may not be true. The race was introduced at the 1896 revival of the Games at the instigation of Michel Breal, a French historian, to commemorate the legendary run of a Greek courier. This man, possibly named Pheidippides, was sent from the village of Marathon, where the Greeks had just defeated a superior Persian invasion army, to Athens with

news of the victory. He is said to have run the 40km (*22 mile*) distance, and crying out, 'Rejoice! We conquer,' collapsed and died. By all accounts he must have been a wonderful runner as he is reported to have previously run to Sparta, about 241km (*150 miles*) away from Athens, to tell them of the invasion and summon help. There is a rather sick joke that has arisen around the story, with the elders of Athens turning to each other and asking, 'What did he say?'

The winner of the marathon at the first modern Olympics in 1896 at Athens was Spiridon 'Spyros' Louis, who had prayed for two days and fasted the day before the race. In addition to the extreme heat the runners had the problem of the dust raised by the numerous accompanying horsemen. As Louis entered the stadium to the excited cheers of his countrymen, the two Greek Royal princes, both tall, strapping men, ran to escort him in, dwarfing his frail figure.

WELL, IF HE CAN DO IT One of the entries for the 1976 Olympic marathon was Waldemar Cierpinski of East Germany, a converted steeplechaser who was virtually unknown even to his own teammates. Author David Wallechinsky, in his *The Complete Book of the Olympics*, notes that the East German soccer team watched the race on television while they were waiting for their final match against Poland. The goalie, Jurgen Croy, was later quoted as saying that the team just stared at each other, thinking that 'if this living example of mediocrity can lift himself to win the marathon, and we don't beat Poland, we will never hear the end of it'. They did beat Poland and won the gold medal. Cierpinski proved that it

was merely a case of having been in the wrong event as he came back four years later, in Moscow, and successfully retained his title.

IT'S ALL RELATIVE In his autobiography the great British marathon runner Jim Peters recounts the story of the 1952 Olympic marathon, in which, though favourite for the title, he failed to finish. The event was won, surprisingly, by the Czech athlete Emil Zatopek, who had already won the 5000m and 10000m and was making his debut at the marathon. Near to halfway, with Peters just leading from Zatopek, the Czech asked if the pace was fast enough. Peters, not feeling very well at all, replied that it was too slow. The triple Olympic champion (he had also won the 10000m in 1948) pondered this for a moment and queried, 'You say "too slow". Are you sure it is too slow?' Peters replied it was, and for a few more strides nothing happened; then Zatopek increased his pace significantly and pulling a Swede with him, soon opened a gap.

Eventually Peters had to drop out but Zatopek went on to win a famous victory, taking over 6 minutes off the Olympic record for the distance. He was well clear of the opposition and was actually eating an apple when the second man, Renaldo Gorno of Argentina, crossed the finishing line. Greeting him with his customary *bonhomie* the Czech pushed the unfinished portion of his apple into Gorno's mouth – and very nearly caused him to expire as he was already gasping for breath after his exertions of the race. Zatopek's feat of winning gold medals at 5000m, 10000m and the marathon at the same championship meeting will probably never be equalled. Lasse Viren of Finland attempted to emulate it in 1976 at Montreal, but after winning the two track races could only finish 5th in the marathon.

MUM'S THE WORD

In her wonderful film of the 1936 Olympics, *Olympische Spiele*, Leni Riefenstahl included some magnificent coverage of marathon running. Although some of her shots were actually filmed afterwards and added for dramatic effect, most of the marathon coverage was live. It included shots of the Japanese entry Kitei Son and the British runner Ernie Harper running mile after mile together and obviously striking up something of a friendship. What was remarkable was that neither spoke the other's language, and Harper noted later that they used hand signals and gestures to indicate how they were feeling and how things were going.

In the race itself the defending champion Juan Zabala of Argentina went off like the proverbial 'bat out of hell' and at one point was over 1½ minutes ahead. Behind him, running in tandem, were Son and Harper, and they remained together until about 16 miles (*28km*) when, with the Argentinian fading badly, Son made his move and took the lead. He eventually won with a new Olympic record time and Harper held onto second place, despite problems with a blistered leg.

Despite being on the programme as representing Japan, Son was in fact an ardent Korean nationalist and felt humiliated by the raising of the Japanese flag during his victory ceremony. Korea at that time was occupied by the Japanese and he and his third-placed teammate, also Korean, were forced to use Japanese names. His Korean name was Sohn Kee-Chung and he insisted on signing autographs like that. He became a national hero and at the 1988 Games, held in Seoul, he was given the honour – at the age of 76, and to a great ovation – of carrying the torch for a short way in the stadium at the Opening Ceremony.

PRECOCIOUS KIDS

Although it is medically recommended that athletes should not run the marathon distance until they are at least 18 years of age, there have been numerous younger runners who have competed, and with distinction. Thus the youngest person to win a national marathon title is Monika Frisch who was still under 13 when she won the Austrian women's title in 1983. Even younger were two American youngsters, a boy of 5 and a girl of 6, who performed very creditably with reported times of just under 5½ hours and 4½ hours respectively.

O YE'LL TAK' THE HIGH ROAD

The highest altitude at which a marathon has started is 5212m (*17100ft*), for the Everest marathon. Needless to say, this race, begun in 1987 and held every two years, runs mainly downhill, ending at a height of 3444m (*11300ft*). The men's record for this event is 3hr59:04 and that for women is 5hr44:32. At the other end of the scale is the Sea of Galilee marathon, which is held on a course 200m (*660ft*) below sea level.

A TASK WORTH DOING

There is a story, perhaps more romantic than factual, about one of the

'Shouldn't you be getting back to your race?'

Italian competitors in the 1908 Olympic marathon in London. Feeling the effects of the heat, he dropped out of the race at about 16 miles. One of the spectators that he talked to was a lady, whom he subsequently married. Settling down in Britain, in 1928 he returned to the course, and restarting at the spot where he had dropped out, he finished the course to the White City stadium.

THE FEMALE OF THE SPECIES

Although the first marathon race ever to be held only occurred early in 1896, the ladies, bless 'em, soon got into the act, albeit unofficially. During that first year there were reports that at least two Greek women had run the distance (at that time 40km): one named Melpomene in about 4½ hours; the other, rather better documented, a mother of seven, Stamatia Rovithi, who clocked 5½ hours. For the next 60 years or so women were barred from competing in marathons, medical advice backing the social mores of the times. However, in the 1960s more and more women began running in the major events, usually in disguise. In the 1966 Boston race Roberta Gibb finished in a respectable 3hr21:40 wearing a hooded garment which kept her hidden from the authorities. The following year Katharine Switzer entered the race by only giving her first initial and received an official number. Although a zealous official physically tried to force her from the race, she did finish it. As the trickle of female runners became a full tide the barriers came down and race after race allowed female competitors.

The best female time on record for the full marathon prior to the 1960s was 3hr40:22 by Britain's Violet Piercy in 1926. That time was not beaten until 1964, but then repeatedly improved upon until the 3 hour barrier went in 1971.

The first major races to accept women officially were those in New York (1971), Boston (1972) and Waldniel, Germany (1973). This latter was the first marathon race to be held solely for women. The first national championships for women were held in the United States (1974) and Germany (1975). International championship races for women were eventually introduced into the European championships (1982), the World championships (1983) and the Olympic Games (1984).

To illustrate the apathy that was met by those pioneering women, the above-mentioned Kathy Switzer tells the story that towards the end of her first Boston marathon she overheard an elderly lady say to her husband, 'Look dearie, isn't that cute? It's a girl and she's wearing earrings.'

HURDLES AND OTHER OBSTACLES

SAMUEL MATETE (1991 World 400m hurdles champion – on how he learnt his technique)

'I just go on one leg. I can't hurdle on the other leg, it's impossible. . . In my picture of Ed Moses he was hurdling on his left leg, so I just copied that'

GREG FOSTER (after winning his third World hurdles title in 1991)

'It felt great and I tried to stay relaxed. I am 32 now. This was the hardest. It really does not get better with age'

KRISS AKABUSI (on the 1987 UK 400m hurdles final, his first major outing at the event)

'I was too close to the first and third, was so far from the fourth and fifth that I had to long-jump them, high-jumped the seventh, clipped the ninth and ran through the tenth. Apart from that, I was immaculate'

ANONYMOUS (suggested quote for the Kenyan steeplechase coach after the 1992 Olympic clean sweep of medals)

'But you should see the three others we left at home'

MOSES KIPTANUI (World record holder – on Kenya's Olympic steeplechase success)

'It has become very important in Kenya to win the steeplechase. We have been winning it since the time of Kipchoge Keino and Amos Biwott, and it has now become a tradition. It is the same as the USA and their sprinters'

SANDRA FARMER-PATRICK (1991 World champion hurdler – on her form)

'I felt like a steeplechaser. I was hopping instead of hurdling'

MARK ROWLAND (British record-holder – about the steeplechase)

'If you make one mistake, it can result in a vasectomy – and I've come pretty close to that before'

PETER McCOLGAN (husband of world 10 000m champion and new mother Liz – asked about his own good form in the steeplechase)

'Well, they say you run better after you've had a baby'

KEVIN YOUNG (1992 Olympic champion)

'I sort of expected to be Olympic champion; but it's going to be hard now every time I open a book or a meeting programme, where it used to say "World record 47.02 Edwin Moses", to see "46.78 Kevin Young". But Ed was the greatest hurdler there's ever been'

HURDLING FASHIONS In the early 1960s a young high hurdler, Denis Waters of Walton AC and the University of London, created a fair amount of interest not so much with his sporting abilities as with his unusual headgear. He invariably ran wearing a Commando-type woolly hat which strongly resembled an item which used to be found in many kitchens. Thus it came as no real surprise to hear an announcement, at the Southern Championships one year, to the effect that 'DB Waters has broken the tea-cosy record.'

GET IT RIGHT In the 1920s a hurdler was disqualified if he knocked down three or more hurdles, while he could not claim a record if he knocked down even one.

Erik Vilen of Finland had set a European 400 metres hurdles record of 55.4s in 1919, when aged 21. In the preliminaries of the event in the 1924 Olympic Games he did not run particularly impressively, only just reaching the final six. The then Olympic record was 54.0, set in 1920, and everyone knew that it would be smashed easily by one of the American competitors, Taylor, Brookins or Riley. Also in the field was the 1908 high jump medallist Georges Andre (France), who had taken the oath for all competitors in the Opening Ceremony of these Games.

When the race was over Vilen had finished in third place but had a silver medal and the Olympic record. What happened was that the winner, Frederick Morgan Taylor, had knocked over a hurdle, and under the rules of the day his time of 52.6 could not be ratified. The second place finisher in 52.8, Charles Brookins, was disqualified for leaving his lane, so Vilen was moved up and his 53.8 became the record.

The 1932 Olympic 400 metres hurdles final was unique in a number of ways. Unusually, it contained four men who were or would become Olympic champions. One of them, Frederick Morgan Taylor, was running in the third final in which he would gain a medal. Another, David Lord Burghley, was the defending champion. The Irishman Robert Tisdall was a virtual novice at the event before going to Los Angeles, and was so tired after his two-week journey to get there that he spent most of his time prior to the race in bed. In the final Tisdall raced into an early lead, and perhaps relaxing too much approaching the last hurdle, knocked it over and nearly fell, but made the line first in 51.8. The American Glen Hardin, in second place, was given the world and Olympic records of 52.0. Hardin went on to win the 1936 final, and in 1934 set a record for the event which lasted for 19 years.

ADVERSITY OVERCOME One of the most remarkable stories in athletics is that of Gail Devers, the American hurdler who won the silver medal in the 1991 World Championships 100m hurdles, breaking the US record in the process. Only six months previously she had faced the possibility of having her feet amputated; it had been discovered that she was suffering from Graves Disease, a thyroid condition which could have caused her death. Happily, after radiation treatment which had terrible side-effects, doctors found a solution to her problem, and though she must take thyroid pills for the rest of her life, she was able to return to training and competition in time to qualify for Tokyo. The following year in the Olympics she fell near the end of the hurdles final but won a gold medal in the flat 100m.

HOME IS BEST John Disley is now better known as one of the organisers of the London marathon, but in his younger days he was an Olympic medallist in the steeplechase. He recalls that on a visit to his native Wales in the mid-fifties he was taken to view the renovations at Cardiff's Maindy Stadium. Quite impressed with most of what he saw, he was more than a little perturbed to be shown the site of the water jump, a gaping hole, and to be informed that it was going to be 'the biggest water jump in the country'. Happily, the information was incorrect.

BIBLE STORIES Runners do not like being nicknamed Moses. It is not for any specific dislike of the name as such, but because what is implied by the donor of the name. In the Bible there is a verse which states, 'God said to Moses, "Go forth",' and the giving of the name is thus applied to runners who just miss out on medals.

While on the subject, there was a double coincidence in the Olympic 400m hurdles at Montreal in 1976 when the American athlete Edwin Moses found himself in races with firstly Jesus Candelo of Columbia and then Jose Jesus Carvalho of Portugal.

WATER JUMP In the steeplechase the water jump consists of a stout 5in (12.7cm) wide hurdle immediately followed by a trough of water, 12ft (3.66m) × 12ft, sloping forward from 2ft 6in (0.7m) deep at the back to ground level at the further end. The normal practice for clearing this obstacle is to place the leading foot on the hurdle, jumping forward so that the other foot lands in a shallow part of the water, with the first foot coming through to land on the dry track, and so back into running with as little break in rhythm as possible.

At the 1968 Olympic Games in Mexico City, the practically unknown Kenyan runner Amos Biwott exhibited his own remarkable style. A virtual novice at the event, who was not listed in the world's top 30 prior to the Games, the 20-year-old Biwott went off at a furious pace in his heat, vastly amusing the crowd by his method of clearing the water obstacle. He did, in fact, just that, leaping from the hurdle clear over the water trough to land on the track – a tiring method which interrupted running cadence and had all the coaches shaking their heads. However, he won the heat and then, amazingly, produced an astonishing sprint at the end of the final to take the gold medal. The explanation offered by Kenyan coach John Velzian for his 'technique' was that 'if you've got only one pair of shoes in the world, you don't want to get them wet'.

AGE SHALL NOT WITHER The British hurdler Don Finlay had an outstanding and long career in an event not noted for longevity. Prior to World War II, he won Olympic silver and bronze medals in the Olympic Games and gold in the Empire Games and European Championships. But perhaps his greatest achievement came at virtually the end of his career. In August 1949, at the exceptional age for a class high hurdler of 40, he beat the 20-year-old American hope Dick Attlesey in a 14.5-second 120y hurdles race at Ibrox Park, Glasgow. The young American was distraught and is reported to have wailed that he couldn't believe that he had been beaten by 'a grandfather', referring to Finlay's very grey hair. Less than a year later Attlesey improved the world record to 13.5.

THE LONGEST STEEPLECHASE? The 1967 International Cross-Country Championship at Barry, Wales, hosted what was probably the longest steeplechase race ever held. The course was over flat grassland and each 1¼ mile (*2000m*) lap contained 2 steeplechase barriers and a water jump. The senior race of 12km comprised six such laps, and the winning time was a very fast 36min 03sec – about 4:49.0 miling pace. Not surprisingly the winner, Gaston Roelants of Belgium, was the reigning Olympic steeplechase champion.

DOUBLE TAKE Only one man has been credited with official world records at both 110m and 400m hurdles. The Swede Sten Pettersson ran the longer distance in 53.8 at Paris in October 1925, and then clocked 14.8 for the high hurdles at Stockholm in 1927. It should be noted that in both cases better times had been achieved in the equivalent Imperial measurement events.

OVERCOME ALL OBSTACLES Older readers will no doubt remember, with mixed feelings, the obstacle races which used to be included in school and holiday camp sports. Climbing over wooden barriers, diving through barrels, hopping from tyre to tyre,

gave rise to a sort of expertise. Perhaps the peak of these skills was epitomised by a fireman, David Harn. The London Fire Brigade held an invitation meeting at the White City in the 1960s, which included a number of standard athletic events with international-class competitors. Also included were some Fire Brigade championships, of which the highlight was an obstacle race. It was held on the grass infield with about eight competitors, qualifiers from local heats. There were the usual obstacles, including a large net or tarpaulin pegged to the ground under which the competitors had to crawl.

The last two items consisted of a large pool of water, naturally filled by a fire engine, followed by a line of beer barrels laid on their side with protective sacking at either end. The soaking wet firemen would dive into their respective barrels to find that it contained a bright coloured dye. The resulting effect brought the house down. No doubt readers will find this all very childish, but there was obviously some considerable skill involved, which brings us back to Mr Harn. After coming second in 1961, he won the event for the next ten years, and who is to say that that run of success should not be bracketed with Arthur Shrubb's ten AAA titles in the early years of the century?

NOTHING SUCCEEDS LIKE SUCCESS Kenyan domination of the steeplechase in recent years has been quite staggering. At the Olympic Games Kenyan runners have won the event since 1968, excluding 1976 and 1980 when their country did not take part. On four of the five occasions left they also won the silver medals, and in 1992 made it a clean sweep. Added to this have been first and second places in the 1991 World championships and their wins in the last three World Junior championships. On the all-time list at the end of 1992 Kenyans held the first six places, while on the 1992 year list there were seven Kenyan runners ranked in the top eight fastest in the world.

SMILE FOR THE BIRDIE The first time that photo-finish equipment was responsible for changing the result of the judges in the Olympic Games was for the 1932 110m hurdles final. The American Jack Keller had been placed third and awarded the bronze medal, but the Kirby Camera photo showed that Britain's Don Finlay had finished fractionally ahead of him. In a fine example of sportsmanship Keller went to the British team's quarters and handed Finlay the medal.

INTERESTING – BUT STUPID
Former British record holder and 400m hurdles champion Harry Kane had one of his most memorable races at the now defunct Sward meeting at Chiswick in the 1950s. Drawn in the outside lane, he found that the hurdles stewards had not been too efficient and while one or two of his hurdles were the wrong height (one too high, another too low), at one point there was no hurdle at all. As he passed friends at the end of the back straight he remarked that this was the most interesting race he had ever run in.

THE JOINT IS JUMPING

MIKE POWELL (1991 World long jump champion – on his goal at Barcelona)

'Nothing less than a gold medal. I've won the silver (in 1988); I'm the world champion and world record holder. There's nowhere for me to go but to the gold medal'

(In fact he won another silver)

AMERICAN SPORTSWRITER (describing a long jumper with little technique)

'He runs for a while, and then takes off'

MIKE POWELL (after long-jumping a world record 8.95m (*29ft 4½in*) at Tokyo in 1991)

'When I came out of the pit I knew at least I had a personal best of 8.80m or something. Then, when I looked at the mark in the sand, I got a little excited'

USA TODAY (headline the day after Mike Powell long-jumped 8.95m at 1991 world championships)

'Powell high-jumps to history'

MIKE HOLMES (British coach recalling his first sighting of Steve Smith, 1992 World Junior high-jump champion and record holder)

'An irritating ginger-haired kid who was always clogging up the high-jump area'

EARL BELL (ex-pole vault world record holder – referring to Sergei Bubka)

'That's the secret of great vaulting. Hold high and carry a big stick'

ISTVAN BAGYULA (Hungarian silver medallist behind Sergei Bubka in 1991 World championships)

'I doubt that anyone could have won this victory. Only Sergei could have lost it'

HOLLIS CONWAY (World Indoor high jump champion – about being heckled by the Cuban crowd at the 1991 Pan-American Games in Havana)

'I've never been whistled at before – except by women'

STEVE SMITH (American world class pole vaulter – 5.61m (*18ft 1in*) in 1975)

'You know, if you put me up 18 feet on a ladder and asked me to jump down into a foam rubber pit, I wouldn't do it'

JAVIER GARCIA (Spanish 5.75m pole vaulter – 1992 Olympic bronze medallist)

'My goal is to be just like Bubka. But to be exactly like him I am lacking a few things: speed, strength, power, and more than anything else – 38cm'

LYNN DAVIES (on his rain-drenched long jump win at the 1964 Olympics)

'If it had been a warm, sunny day in Tokyo I wouldn't have won the gold, I know that. I've got to be very honest about that. The Welsh gods must have been in Tokyo'

RESTRICTIVE PRACTICES AT THE BAR In 1954, when the world high jump record was only 2.12m (*6ft 11½in*), an American Dick Browning reportedly cleared a bar set at 2.28m (*7ft 6in*). The problem was that he was the US Tumbling champion and made his clearance with a somersault at the end of a tumbling sequence. The rules prohibited such a method of clearance. The world record at the end of 1992 stood at 2.44m (*8ft 0in*) and virtually all world-class jumpers use the flop style in which the athlete turns and clears the bar on his back – a far cry from the restrictive rules of the past. However, the regulations still specify that a jumper may not use a double-footed take-off, so tumblers are still barred.

In the 1930s it was forbidden for high jumpers to clear a bar head first, or with a diving action. In the days of hard sand surfaces this was as much a matter of safety as of aesthetics. At the 1932 Olympic Games the women's high jump title was being fought out between two Americans, Jean Shiley and Mildred Didrikson. The latter, unusually, used a roll-like action in which her head often preceded her body. Both women had tied for first

The outlook is bright for Davies

place and took part in a jump-off. Still they were tied. Then suddenly, in one of the most ludicrous decisions ever made in the event, the judges declared Didrikson's style inadmissible and awarded the gold medal to Shiley. Didrikson, who had been using the same style throughout the competition, was given the silver medal, although one could have argued that she should have been disqualified altogether. Even more strangely, she was given credit, with Shiley, for the world record they had set in the main competition.

At the Olympic Games of 1936, Dorothy Odam of Great Britain cleared the same height (1.60m) as the winner, but was placed second. Twelve years later she again jumped the same height as the winner (1.68m) and again was placed second. Ironically, if the rules in force in 1948 had been in force in 1936, she would have won at Berlin; and if the reverse had been true she would have had the gold medal at London!

In July 1988, 24-year-old Yan Zhi-cheng, a member of the Chinese State Circus touring Holland, jumped cleanly through a hoop, the lowest edge of which was measured as 2.46m (*8ft 0¾in*) above the ground. This jump, at The Hague, was one of over 100 such jumps claimed by Yan as part of his act. His technique involves a two-footed jump head-first through a series of hoops, set one upon another, with the highest one being at the height noted above.

TEACHER AND PUPILS Since the modern Olympics began in 1896, American pole vaulters have won 17 gold, 12 silver and 11 bronze medals. The highest placing by a British vaulter has been a shared sixth place in 1936.

It is therefore salutary to note that an Englishman, Tom Ray, was instrumental in popularising the event in the United States when he went there in 1887 and won their national title. Two years later another member of Ray's Ulverstone Cricket and Football Club, Ernest Stones, also won the US title. In those days a 'climbing' technique was used and athletes from Lancashire dominated. In 1889 the style was banned in the United States and in 1919 Great Britain followed. Since the introduction of modern techniques, the pole vault has been one of the weakest events for Britain in major international competition.

> **BRIGITTE BARDOT** (*advice to potential 1968 Olympic athletes after making a film in Mexico City*)
>
> *'GET THERE EARLY, REST A FEW DAYS, TRAIN CAREFULLY, AND CUT DOWN ON YOUR ROMANCE UNTIL YOU GET USED TO THE ALTITUDE'*

GENTLY DOES IT When winning the 1991 Australian pole vault championship with a new record of 5.55m, Simon Arkell became the latest exponent of a questionable, but legal, practice in the event. He actually dislodged the bar, but as he passed over it he replaced it back on the uprights. The technique is thought to have been invented by the American Dave Volz a few years before.

The American high jumper Harold Osborn, who won the Olympic event in 1924, caused the high jump rules to be changed by his habit of pressing the bar back against the uprights while using his western roll technique. After this the bar was set so as to fall freely in either direction.

THE POWER OF THE MIND?

When Ni Chih Chin of China set a world high jump mark of 2.29m in 1970 he was quoted as saying that, 'If my jumps were as high as the thoughts of Chairman Mao, I would need a fireman's ladder to measure them.' Coincidentally the record he broke was held by Valeriy Brumel (URS) who was born on exactly the same day, 14 April 1942, as the Chinese jumper.

ALL STYLES ARE GOOD EXCEPT THE TIRESOME SORT

Voltaire's statement of 1738 might well apply to high jumping today. With about 99.9% of jumpers using the Fosbury technique, competitions can sometimes be quite boring. Although the heights cleared thirty years ago were perhaps 30–35cm less, there were numerous styles used which made competitions more entertaining. Often one could see exponents of the Straddle, Western Roll, Eastern Cut-off and Modified Scissors all in the same event, whereas today one rarely sees any of these. Indeed, there is reason to believe that some jumpers would benefit more from one of the older styles than they do from the Fosbury, but few coaches could or would teach them.

JUMPING JACKS (& JILLS) The current world records for the men and women's high jumps are 2.44m (*8ft 0in*) and 2.09m (*6ft 10¼in*) respectively. However, there is a good argument to be made that the holders of these records are not the best high jumpers ever. It has been suggested that a greater measure of a high jumper's ability is the height he clears in relation to his own height. The current record

holders, Javier Sotomayor of Cuba (1.95m tall) and Stefka Kostadinova of Bulgaria (1.80m), have, by this method, jumped 49cm and 29cm above their heads. In 1978 an American athlete, Franklin Jacobs, cleared 2.32m (*7ft 7¼in*) which was a record 59cm above his own height, while in 1990 a countrywoman of his, Yolanda Henry, set a female record, jumping 2.00m (*6ft 6¾in*) which was 32cm over her head.

PUTTING ON THE STYLE Sir Arthur Gold is a well-known figure in British and world sports circles, having been Chairman of the British Olympic Association, President of the European Athletic Association and Hon. Secretary of the British Amateur Athletic Board. However, back in the late 1930s he was an international high jumper using the difficult but technically excellent Eastern Cut-off technique. Later to become a coach, he was rather proud of his style; but in a story that he tells against himself, that pride was shattered somewhat at a meeting in Stockholm in September 1937. He was competing against the holder of the world record (2.09m) Mel Walker of the USA, who proceeded to win the competition easily with 2.00m, while Arthur cleared 1.80m. Afterwards Walker came over to him and said, 'Arthur, I sure like your style; but I sure like my height better.'

METHINKS IT WERE AN EASY LEAP (*Henry IV, Part I*) In August 1901 Peter O'Connor of Ireland broke his own world long jump best with a leap of 7.61m (*24ft 11¾in*) in Dublin. That mark remained as the official world record for 20 years (less 13 days).

However it remained as an Irish record for nearly 89 years until broken in June 1990. No national record in a standard event has lasted as long.

The mark of 8.13m (*26ft 8¼in*) set by Jesse Owens (USA) on his 'day of days', 25 May 1935, was not bettered for a record 25 years until August 1960. Bob Beamon's famous jump of 8.90m (*29ft 2½in*) in the rarefied atmosphere of Mexico City during the 1968 Olympic Games lasted for over 21 years, until the 1991 World championships at Tokyo.

ONE WAY OR ANOTHER

Perhaps the most unusual switch of events occurred at the 1924 Olympic Games. Charlie Hoff of Norway arrived in Paris as the world record holder in the pole vault (4.21m) but had to withdraw from that event due to an injury. However, being an athlete of wide-ranging abilities, he entered the 400m and 800m events, reaching the final of the latter.

CAPTAIN, WHERE ART THOU

In 1954 Charles Van Dyck, then studying law in London and one of the best high jumpers in the country, was selected as team captain for Ghana at the British Empire & Commonwealth Games in Vancouver, Canada. His brother, who was living in America, had read about this in a Ghanaian paper and made the journey especially to see him. Unfortunately, Charles was not in Vancouver – due to a mix-up he was never even told that he was in the team, and stayed in London.

STAND AND DELIVER

In the 19th century and the first part of the 20th, standing jumps were very popular. In these the athlete had to stand with feet together before he jumped, the only prior movement allowed being of the torso or arms. The interest was such that high jump, long jump and triple jump by this method were included in the Olympic Games of 1900 and 1904, and the first two were also contested in the Games up to 1912. The superstar of this technique was Ray Ewry (USA) who won a record 10 gold medals between 1900 and 1908, and was undefeated in Olympic competition. He had developed tremendous leg strength while recovering from childhood polio.

The events are rarely contested today outside Scandinavia. The current acknowledged bests for the events are:

Men

HJ ... 1.90m (*6ft 2¾in*) ...... Rune Almen (SWE) 1980
LJ .... 3.71m (*12ft 2¼in*) .... Arne Tvervaag (NOR) 1968

Women

HJ ... 1.52m (*4ft 11¾in*) .... Grete Bjordalsbakke (NOR) . 1984
LJ .... 2.92m (*9ft 7in*) .... Annelin Mannes (NOR) 1981

AND A RIGHT GOOD CAPTAIN, TOO (WS Gilbert HMS Pinafore) The captain of the Irish team in the Triangular International against England and Scotland in 1947 was Prince Adegboyega Adedoyin. A Nigerian high/long jumper, he was then studying medicine at Queen's University, Belfast, and won three events for his team, including a hurdles win over Don Finlay. A fine all-rounder, he twice won four Irish titles, in 1947 and 1948. In the latter year he also represented Great Britain in the Olympic Games in the high and long jumps.

HIGH AND MIGHTY The greatest winning streak ever achieved in the sport was achieved by Iolanda Balas of Romania in the high jump. From December 1956 to June 1967 she won 140 consecutive competitions, usually by big margins. Basically using a modified version of the old-fashioned scissors jump, Balas, who was 1.85m (6ft 1in) tall – most of that being legs – dominated her event during that period in a way that has rarely been equalled. During this time she won two European titles and two Olympic gold medals, and set 14 world records (itself a record) between 1956 (1.75m) and 1961 (1.91). The latter mark stood for just over 10 years.

JUMP TO IT Victor Saneyev of the Soviet Union was one of the greatest athletic champions of all time, but he was unfortunately overshadowed by the great American discus thrower Al Oerter. Oerter's claim to fame, and one that will probably never be surpassed, is his four Olympic victories from 1956–68. Saneyev

may well have a greater claim, especially so in an event notorious for its catalogue of injuries, the triple jump. He won three consecutive Olympic titles from 1968–76 and then placed a close second in 1980 when nearly 35 years of age. During the period from 1968 to 1977 he won 96 of his 110 competitions, a quite superb record. His first love had been the high jump, but an early injury had caused him to look elsewhere.

HIGH, HIGHER, HIGHEST? There have been many strange results in athletics, but surely few could match what happened at the Hertfordshire County championships in the early 1960s. John Leavold of St Albans City club won the high jump, as expected, with a clearance of 1.85m (6ft 1in), and then proceeded to take the pole vault title with a height of 1.83m (6ft 0in).

JUMPING JACKS The Olympic triple jump competition at Mexico City in 1968 was unique in that more world records were set during it than in any other competition in history. In the qualifying round Giuseppe Gentile of Italy added 7cm to the existing record. The following day in the final, he improved to 17.22m in the first round. In the third round, defending champion Victor Saneyev of the Soviet Union added another centimetre. Two rounds later Nelson Prudencio of Brazil took the record to 17.27m to regain a record that his countryman Ferreira da Silva had held in the 1950s. Then in the last round Saneyev grabbed it back with a leap of 17.39m. Although the rarefied air of Mexico City obviously helped, a number of expert observers said that a general improvement in the technical standard of the jumpers was as much the reason.

TOLD YOU SO In 1932 high jumper Duncan MacNaughton was only selected for Canada's Olympic team for Los Angeles because he was already at college at the University of Southern California. Against all the odds he won the gold medal with a jump of 1.97m (*6ft 5½in*). He was helped considerably by the coaching advice of his University teammate Robert Van Osdel (USA) who placed second.

Robert LeGendre failed to make the American team for the long jump in 1924 but did qualify for the athletic pentathlon event. At the Paris Olympics, competing the day before the long jump final proper, LeGendre jumped 7.76m (*25ft 5¾in*) to break the world record. He eventually finished third in the pentathlon. The long jump event was won with only 7.44m and indeed LeGendre's jump was not surpassed in the Olympics until 1936.

IF YOU WANT TO GET AHEAD, GET A HAT In 1876 the Hon. Marshall Brooks raised the world high jump record first to 6ft 0in (*1.83m*) and then to 6ft 2½in (*1.89m*). When Brooks, an Oxford undergraduate, turned up at the English championships that year he had no rivals for the title and won it by clearing 6ft 0in reputedly still wearing his top hat.

American 800m runner Dave Wottle became a familiar sight on world athletics tracks in the early 1970s wearing an old gold cap –

his lucky charm. He won the US title in 1972 and then in the Olympic trials equalled the world mark of 1.44.3. However, due to his comparative lack of experience and a recent injury, he was not a favourite for the gold medal. In the final, with 200m to go he was lying 8th and last. With a devastating burst he just pushed his chest to the title by a mere 3/100ths of a second from Yevgeniy Arzhanov of the Soviet Union, who stumbled a metre or so from the finishing line and fell. The excitement of winning was so great that Wottle went to the victory ceremony still wearing his cap and totally forgot to take it off during the playing of the American anthem. It was only when reporters questioned him afterwards that he realised what he had done, and nearly in tears, he made a formal apology via the media to the American people.

OPPORTUNITY KNOCKS Irving Baxter (USA) won the high jump at the 1900 Olympic Games in Paris, and about 1 hour later had also won the pole vault. The three better American vaulters had either refused to compete because the event was held on a Sunday or had been wrongly informed that the event was to be re-scheduled. The following year Baxter turned up for the AAA championships without a pole, and when no-one would lend him one he literally pulled up a flagpole and used it; he tied for the title.

UNUSUAL DOUBLING It is not uncommon for long jumpers to excel in other events, sprints and hurdles especially, but sometimes they surprise elsewhere. Perhaps the best example of this was Japan's female superstar of the

1920s Kinue Hitomi. When she went to the Olympic Games she was world record holder in the long jump. However, there was no such event for women at the Games in those days, so she ran in the 800m and won the silver medal. Another unusual combination was that of Jose Telles da Conceicao of Brazil, who won the high jump silver medal in the 1952 Games and returned four years later to place 6th in the 200m.

The only man to win Olympic titles in both long and triple jumps was Myer Prinstein (USA). Having won the triple in 1900 he only gained the silver in the long jump, but made up for it in 1904 at St Louis, winning both events.

GO STRAIGHT TO GOAL The only full British soccer international to reach the 'heights' in national athletics was the amateur player B Howard Baker of Chelsea and the Corinthians in the 1920s. Twice he was goalkeeper for England and in 1921, representing Liverpool Harriers, he set a high jump record of 6ft 5in (*1.956m*) which was not bettered by a Briton for 25 years.

VIVE LA DIFFERENCE In 1938 Dora Ratjen of Germany set world records in the women's high jump with 1.66m, 1.67m and 1.70m. She also won the European championship of that year. Dora then disappeared – and reappeared some 14 years later in Bremen as a waiter named Hermann. He insisted that he had not intended to cheat but that the Nazis had forced him to pose as a woman from 1936 till the War, 'for the honour and glory of the Fatherland'. He said, 'For three

years I lived the life of a girl. It was most dull.' After the war his records were expunged and Britain's Dorothy Odam-Tyler had her mark of 1.66m in 1939 retrospectively accepted.

LONG, LONGER, LONGEST?
The introduction of League athletics to Britain in the 1960s really brought home to clubs the importance of loyalty among their members, particularly in clubs which did not have members with skills in some of the more technical events. This led to some pretty poor results in events such as the pole vault, discus, hammer and javelin. Perhaps this was brought home best by the efforts of a member of the Polytechnic Harriers in a match at Twickenham in May 1969. Nick Overhead had been an international 400m runner in the early 1960s but was only too willing to help his club out in a variety of events. Thus he long jumped a creditable 6.77m (*22ft 2½in*) at the meeting and barely exceeded that distance with the hammer, in which he achieved 7.08m (*23ft 3in*)

TUCKED UP NICE AND SAFE
The athletics world was shaken in 1973 when reports came from Germany of an athlete named Bernhard Stierle who was doing a somersault long jump. In this style the jumper curls into the tuck position (similar to a high diver) to minimise drag, or wind resistance. He then unrolls himself to extend his feet fully to land. Early reports from Germany and New Zealand, where John Delamere eventually reached 7.79m (*25ft 6¾in*), suggested that it might catch on, but horrified by the potential dangers, the IAAF banned it in

1974. Since then it has come to light that an athlete at a Minnesota high school tried the style back in the 1950s.

EAT YOUR HEART OUT, CARL LEWIS

During the 19th century in Britain a number of professional 'jumpers' became quite famous, performing on the halls and in clubs. Perhaps the best known was Joe Darby of Staffordshire, who gave an exhibition by Royal Command before the Prince of Wales (later King Edward VII) in November 1888. Described as a man of great modesty and charm, he is said to have made a standing long jump of 12ft 1½in (3.69m) in 1890, and to have reached 14ft 9in (4.49m), using hand weights, at the Star Music Hall in Liverpool a few months later. One of his more esoteric 'tricks' was to jump onto the surface of water in a tank and out again, only wetting the soles of his shoes. A contemporary, John Higgins of Blackburn, was reputed to be able to jump into a case of eggs placed on a chair and then jump over the back of the chair to the floor with not an egg broken (members of the audience checked the eggs before and after the performance). In May 1854 John Howard of Chester leaped 29ft 7 in (9.02m) at Chester, using dumb-bells and taking off from a slightly raised block of wood.

CHEEK, EFFRONTERY?

Most dictionaries find the Yiddish word 'chutzpah' is very difficult to define. One of the best illustrations of the word in athletics was the performance of Britain's Dalton Grant in the 1991 World championships in Tokyo. Throughout the preceding months he had great difficulty exceeding 2.20m, well short of his British record 2.34m of the previous year. His best pre-championships performance was 2.30m, and that on only one occasion. His Tokyo qualifying jump of 2.27m, along with 13 others, indicated nothing special.

In the final, all the others entered the competition at 2.24m but to the horror of all his supporters Grant did not come in till the bar was raised to 2.31m. This he proceeded to clear on his first jump, for a season's best. Elation was replaced by consternation in the British camp when he then passed at the next height of 2.34m (equal to his record).

With the bar at 2.36m Grant failed his first two jumps and recriminations were already flowing when he sailed over on his third and last attempt for a new British mark. There were now only four jumpers left. Unhappily, he could not clear 2.38m and was placed fourth on the count-back rule.

It transpired that he had a foot injury and knew he had to keep his jumps to a minimum.

THROWING THEIR WEIGHT ABOUT

FATIMA WHITBREAD (former world champion and record-holder in the javelin)

'I know I don't look like Kim Basinger, but then Kim Basinger can't throw the javelin'

DANA ZATOPKOVA (1952 Olympic javelin champion – on rumours of a new style of throwing in the 1950s)

'If this new method is accepted I will personally break my javelin and use it as a support for tomato plants'

AL OERTER (four-time Olympic discus champion – on his injuries and their probable effect on his chances for a fourth gold)

'These are the Olympics – you die for them'

HOMER (Greek epic poet)

'THERE IS NO GREATER GLORY FOR A MAN AS LONG AS HE LIVES THAN THAT WHICH HE WINS BY HIS OWN HANDS AND FEET'

A WINNING STREAK Canadian shot put exponent George Gray held the world record from 1888 till 1904, and as a member of the famous New York AC, won 10 US championships. He was also undefeated for a period of 13 years, 1885–98.

A successor in the shot, Parry O'Brien (USA), also had a remarkable series of wins over a much shorter period. Between July 1952 and June 1956 O'Brien won 116 consecutive competitions, including the 1952 Olympic title. After his streak was ended he successfully defended his Olympic title at Melbourne, added a silver medal in 1960 and returned again in 1964 to gain fourth place at Tokyo.

Women throwers have also created some enviable series of successive victories, usually in careers with fewer opportunities for competition. Nadyezda Chizhova, the Soviet shot star, won 57 competitions from 1969–73 while her compatriot Faina Melnik won 52 discus events from 1973–76. Even better was Germany's Gisela Mauermayer who had 65 consecutive wins in the discus from 1935–42, although this was a period of less international competition.

However, the greatest winning streak of all time was that of 140 by Romanian high jumper Iolanda Balas from December 1956 to June 1967. The best by a male, and the best by a track athlete, was 122 by Edwin Moses (USA) in the 400m hurdles from August 1977 to June 1987. His career record was 178 wins out of 187 races from 1975 to 1988.

BETTER LATE THAN NEVER
One athlete who literally 'missed the boat' was Britain's Tom Nicholson, a Scottish farmer and Olympic hammer thrower, who failed to catch the team boat to Antwerp in 1920. He arrived after the hammer qualifying round had been contested, but the other

competitors insisted that he should be allowed to compete in the final. He did and finished in sixth place.

BUT THEIR NAME LIVETH FOR EVERMORE (*Ecclesiasticus*) Not many athletes have places named after them and perhaps the most successful in this way was Etienne Desmarteau of Canada. A Montreal policeman, he was one of only two non-Americans to win an athletic title in the 1904 Olympic Games at St Louis when he took the 56lb weight throw event. He died the following year aged only 32 of typhoid and a park was named in his honour in his home city.

OLD HABITS DIE HARD When Steve Backley threw the javelin 91.46m (*300ft 1in*) for a new world record at Auckland in January 1992, the press reports all noted that he used the recently-standardised smooth javelin. For the previous 12 months or so a 'rough-ended' model had been in use which had taken the 'record' past 96 metres, but now the governing body had outlawed that and everything in the garden was lovely. However, all this was put into some sort of perspective by a letter to *The Times* which noted that surely what was most important about Backley's throw was the fact that he became the first with the official javelin to throw over 100 yards.

DEAR EARTH, I SALUTE THEE (*Richard II*) A member of a touring under-23 athletics team from Australia dug up the area of Auckland turf where Backley's

spear had landed, as a memento. Rather harshly commenting on the stupidity of this act, a New Zealand journalist commented, 'As if they don't have enough clods in Australia already.'

THE LIGHT THAT LED ASTRAY (*Robert Burns*) The London newspaper *The Evening News* sponsored a number of meetings in the 1950s which primarily consisted of matches between London and other strong athletic cities such as Stockholm, Moscow and Budapest. At these meetings endeavours were made to introduce some new events and perhaps the best remembered of these was the 'Flaming Hammer' competition in the London v Budapest meeting of October 1956.

The Hungarians had three superb throwers in their team, Josef Csermak, Gyula Zsivotsky and Imre Nemeth, while London was represented by Peter Allday and Don Anthony. In an attempt to make it more of a spectacle, it was arranged for the event to be held when nothing else was going on in the stadium. Most of the lights were turned off and a sparkler firework was attached to each hammer head prior to the throw – the idea being that the crowd could follow the graceful arc of light. It worked very well until near the end of the competition.

It should be noted that because the British competitors, throwing alternately with the Hungarians, were not as good as their opposition, the judges invariably had to move three or four metres nearer to the throwing circle whenever they measured their throws. Usually they only moved back part of the way for the visitors' throws, but ordinarily this was not dangerous because they could follow the arc of light easily

'Our anti-aircraft system includes
surface-to-air discoi . . .'

enough and gauge where the implement was going to land.

However, one of the Hungarians made his throw, and according to the light from the firework the trajectory suddenly veered sharply down to the ground. In the gloom, spectators could dimly see the judges running forward to mark the landing spot – when realisation dawned. The sparkler had fallen off! Somewhere up above them was a death-dealing 16lb ball attached to a 3ft chain. There were loud cries of dismay and the crowd watched as normally staid British officials scattered in all directions. Happily nothing except pride was dented and the stadium rocked with relieved laughter. Understandably, the experiment was not tried again.

AHOY, THERE In the late 1960s a number of good discus throws were reported for Britain's Bill Tancred, with the venue shown as HMS *Ganges*. This caused some speculation that it must be an aircraft-carrier and further discussion as to how many discoi were lost overboard. It eventually came to light that HMS *Ganges* was a Royal Navy shore base near Ipswich.

OUCH! According to *The Santa Barbara News-Press*, an American javelin thrower turned up at the local stadium in 1991 trying to get a qualifying mark for the forthcoming world championships. Apparently a number of spectators were milling around on the field as the competition was due to start, prompting the Santa Barbara coach to announce, 'If you get stuck by the javelin, we're going to leave it in you until we measure it.'

IT FELL TO EARTH, I KNOW NOT WHERE During the Festival of Britain in 1951 on London's South Bank, one of the many displays was an exhibition of hammer-throwing conducted by the then National Coach, Geoff Dyson. Helping him was Major Charles Reidy, a noted thrower of the time. A thick rope safety 'cage' was set up around the stage on which the display was being held, even though no actual throwing was intended. With Dyson providing a commentary, Reidy demonstrated the technique of the event to a fairly large, appreciative crowd. However, after showing examples of one turn and then two turns, Major Reidy then did three turns and let the hammer fly, gently he thought, into the ropes. Perhaps the ropes were defective, but the hammer tore its way straight through them, and sailed away over the heads of the spectators, towards the main concourse which was thronged with people.

An ashen-faced Dyson and helpers rushed to see what carnage and havoc had been caused and were surprised, but extremely thankful, to find no commotion nor injured people at all. Indeed, they could not even find the hammer. After some searching it was finally discovered embedded and twisted into two bicycles leaning against a small tree alongside the pathway. With considerable difficulty they extricated the implement and scurried away, leaving the owners to wonder what sort of horrific occurrence could have mangled their bikes in such a fashion.

SAVING THE BEST TILL LAST The Czech javelin thrower Jan Zelezny arrived in Oslo for the Grand Prix in 1992 surrounded by rumours that he was ready to throw a 'big one'. He had set a world mark in Oslo two years previously and was now using the new Nemeth javelin which was supposed to add several metres to a good throw. All eyes were on him for his first throw, delivered with his usual ferocity – only for it to travel a ludicrous 7–8m. It transpired that the implement had slipped through his hand. His next four throws all improved on the previous one (!) with the fifth only a few centimetres short of the world mark of 91.46m set by Steve Backley earlier in the year. With his last throw, in customary fashion throwing himself to the ground with the effort, Zelezny improved the record by a massive 3.28m. Later in the year, using an 'ordinary' javelin, he won the Olympic gold medal.

DAY OF DAYS At Rehlingen, Germany on 19 May 1975, Karl-Hans Riehm bettered the listed world record for the hammer with all six of his throws. Such a series of performances is unique in the annals of the sport.

A PARTING SHOT In the Middle Ages putting the weight was such a popular pastime in the English countryside that King Edward III issued an edict banning it. Apparently he feared it was interfering with archery practice, a very necessary pastime for the defence of the realm. There has always been some doubt as to whether that edict was ever repealed. If not it raises the terrible spectre of British record holder Geoff Capes, a policeman during his long, illustrious career, breaking the law every time he competed.

IT'S WARMER, TOO A research project conducted by the National Physical Laboratory some years ago indicated that because the Earth is flattened at the Poles, the gravitational pull is less at the Equator. It was postulated that a shot put of 60ft (*18.29m*) at the North Pole would travel 3½in (*9cm*) further if duplicated at the Equator.

WHEN THE SNOW LAY ROUND ABOUT A throwing-the-snowball competition has been held annually since 1972 at Pöytyä in southern Finland, and is a popular part of the Finnish Shrovetide (Lent) celebrations. The event attracts many of the best Finnish javelin throwers, who are among the best in the world. The balls are made by a machine and are quite large, being about 10cm in diameter and 300–400 grams in weight. Having a big hand is a definite advantage. The men's record is 93.60m by Jorma Markus in 1980, while the best by a woman is 66.56m by the only foreigner ever to have taken part, Karin Smith (USA) in 1992. It is reported that the organisers are planning to broaden the competition to 'World Championship' level.

HEADS DOWN One of the best javelin throwers of thirty years or so ago was Bill Alley of the United States. He threw the implement a personal best of 83.48m in 1960. However, perhaps his best throw was not with a javelin, but with a 3lb hand grenade which he is reported to have thrown a record distance of 90.84m (*298ft*).

It is interesting to note that a 'Throwing-the-Hand-Grenade'

event was included in the Soviet Championships for men and women from 1927 to 1946. It was normally won, as one would expect, by javelin throwers.

The equivalent event in Great Britain was, of course, throwing the cricket ball, and it was a staple event in school sports until the 1950s. The greatest distance ever achieved with a cricket ball (5½oz/155g) was reported as 422ft (*128.60m*) by left-handed thrower Robert Percival at Durham Sands racecourse on Easter Monday 1882. A few modern throwers have tried for this 'record' and the nearest anyone has come was the 126.52m (*415ft*) thrown by British javelin international Mick Hill.

'I said, Mind how you go with that pin, comrade'

AND THICK AND FAST
THEY CAME AT LAST

(Lewis Carroll)

MARY PETERS (1972 Olympic pentathlon champion – on her practical father)

'For my 16th birthday I got a ton of sand for a sandpit so I could high jump, and for my 17th birthday a load of cement. It was the first shot circle ever laid in Ireland'

CLOVA COURT (British heptathlete – on her attitude to rivals)

'I'm out to beat them and they are out to beat me. It is as simple as that. I will say hello to them at a meeting but I don't phone them up for friendly chats or anything like that. I keep myself to myself. If that sounds selfish, so be it'

O FRABJOUS DAY (*Lewis Carroll***)** On 25 May 1935 at Ann Arbor, Michigan, on the occasion of the Western Athletic Conference ('Big Ten') championships, Jesse Owens set six world records within the space of an hour. Strangely, Owens, representing Ohio State University, was in such pain from a strained back, incurred in a friendly game of touch-football earlier in the week, that his coach Larry Snyder wanted to withdraw him from the meet. After some discussion it was decided that Jesse would try the 100y, which came first, and see how his back reacted. His time of 9.4 equalled the world mark – and three unofficial watches were a tenth faster.

He then went to the long jump pit and with his first and only jump he broke the world record by 15cm (*6in*), clearing 8.13m (*26ft 8¼in*). That record was to last for over 25 years. Just 15 minutes later he lined up for the 220y, held on a straightaway, a common occurrence in the United States at that time. In this race he ran 20.3, a 0.3 second improvement on the world standard held by his friend Ralph Metcalfe.

Although he was feeling a little tired, Owens now asked coach Snyder if he could also try the 220y hurdles, an event he did not often train for let alone run. Snyder, caught up in the euphoria, said yes, and Owens lined up with some of the best low hurdlers of the day. He admits in his autobiography that suddenly he had doubts and seriously considered dropping out, claiming his back was hurting. Then he thought of Charles Riley, his high school coach, who had set him on his way, and who had told him, 'Never forget this: there's bound to come a time in your life when you'll be asked for more than ability. When that happens, you'll have to make up the difference – in manhood.' He stayed in the race and 22.6 seconds later was the new record holder.

It was sensational – world records in four events, and the IAAF also recognised his times as records for the intermediate distances of 200m and 200m hurdles, so raising his record total to 6. Almost as soon as he was finished with his afternoon efforts, his backache came back and it is reported that his team-mates had to help him onto the team bus. It is worth noting that starting blocks were not allowed at that time.

THE OLIVER TWIST SYNDROME One of the great runners of the 19th century, Lawrence 'Lon' Myers (USA) won the 100y, 220y, 440y and 880y at the 1880 American championships, all on the same afternoon. Britain's Wyndham Halswelle, the 1908 Olympic 400m champion, won the same four events at the 1906 Scottish championships, also on the one day.

A contemporary of Myers, the great English runner Walter George, won the 880y, 1 mile and 4 mile titles on one day at the 1884 AAA championships, and then two days later also took the national 10 mile crown.

The greatest number of AAA outdoor titles won is 15 by Emmanuel McDonald Bailey of Trinidad, with 7 at 100y, 7 at 220y, and 1 relay, between 1946 and 1953. The most WAAA outdoor titles is 14 by Suzanne Allday, with 7 in the shot and 7 in the discus, between 1952 and 1961. Including indoor championships Judy Oakes won a total of 30 national titles (10 WAAA outdoor, 12 WAAA indoor, 8 UK) between 1977 and 1991, all in the shot.

The greatest number of American national titles won is 65 by Ron Laird in various walking events, indoor and outdoor, between 1958 and 1976.

In the 1954 Ceylon championships, the Olympic pole vault champion, Rev. Bob Richards (USA) took part in eight events, winning six and placing second in another. One afternoon in 1907 at the Canadian championships, Walter Knox – later (in 1914) to become Britain's first national coach – won the 100y, long jump, pole vault, shot

and hammer. On another non-championship occasion he had notched ten first places at the one meeting.

Although there have been a number of athletes who have won multiple gold medals at one celebration of the Olympic Games, perhaps the greatest feat was that of the Czech distance runner Emil Zatopek in 1952. He first won the 10000m in Olympic record time. Two days later he ran a heat of the 5000m and two days after that he won that title as well, also in a new record time. Three days later he won his first ever marathon, yet again setting a new Olympic record.

VERSATILITY There have been many examples of athletes who had a wide spread of excellence in a number of events, not least among women. However, one of the more outstanding was Kinue Hitomi of Japan in the 1920s. When the first women's events were held at the Olympics in 1928 she held the world records in the 200m and long jump. As neither of these events were in the Olympic schedule she entered the 800m, and won the silver medal. In her short career (she unfortunately died aged 23) she set Japanese records in nine different events, including the discus and javelin.

AND WHAT IS SO RARE AS A DAY IN JUNE? (*James Russell Lowell*) The great Finnish runner Paavo Nurmi achieved perhaps his ultimate on 19 June 1924 at Helsinki. He first ran 3:52.6 to beat the previous world record for 1500m by 2.1 seconds, a margin only bettered once since. Within less than an hour he had also broken the world record for 5000m with 14:28.2, by a margin of 7.2 seconds. He was using these runs as a test for the same Olympic double on 10 July in Paris. There he again won both events within 1½ hours, both in Olympic record times.

THE GREATEST One of the more extreme larger-than-life characters to grace athletics was Jim Thorpe, one of the best all-round athletes and sportsmen that the world has ever seen. Although he is better known in America as one of the all-time greats at their code of football, he has entered athletics legend with his performances at the 1912 Olympic Games at Stockholm.

Thorpe was born of American Indian parents in Oklahoma and given the Indian name of Wa-Tho-Huck (Bright Path). He was actually a twin but his brother, who was rather sickly, died at the age of 10. Further tragedy struck when his mother died two years later and his father just three years after that. It was while he was at the Carlisle Indian School that his sporting prowess came to the fore, and he was nurtured by the athletics coach 'Pop' Warner. Although football was his first love – he led the school to some astounding victories including one against Harvard University – he was also making headlines on the track. One of his most memorable days was when he represented Carlisle against another college with only one other athlete, Lewis Tewanima, a distance runner, for company. Out of nine events entered he won seven, and the match.

At Stockholm he began by winning the pentathlon, then an athletics event comprising the long jump, javelin, 200m, discus and

1500m. He finished first in all but the javelin (third) and won the title by a record margin of 14 points. The following day he participated in the individual high jump and placed equal fourth. He rested for five days and then competed in the individual long jump, placing seventh. The decathlon started on the same day. (In 1912 it was contested over three days, instead of the normal two.)

On the first day there were three events, with four on the second and three on the third. Thorpe recorded first place in four events (shot, high jump, 110m hurdles and 1500m), placed third in four more and was fourth in two. It is interesting to note that prior to leaving for the Games, in a high jump competition, he had beaten the world record holder Horine and the man who was to win the Olympic title, Richards. Soon after the Games he beat the Olympic 110m hurdles champion in a very fast time.

When the medals were awarded at Stockholm, King Gustav of Sweden said to him, 'Sir, you are the greatest athlete in the world.' To which Thorpe is said to have replied, 'Thanks, King.' Unfortunately, early the following year it was revealed that he had played minor professional baseball, which by the rules made him ineligible to compete at the Olympics. Despite pleas that he was a simple Indian boy who did not know of the ramifications of such action, the US governing body took a very hard line and his name and deeds were expunged from the results and the record books. A ludicrously severe policy, albeit legal in the light of all the facts. To their eternal credit, the Norwegian and Swede who were awarded his first place in the pentathlon and decathlon respectively, refused to accept the gold medals.

Totally disillusioned, Thorpe played professional baseball and football until 1928. During the 1930s he drifted from job to job, the one highspot being when he was invited by the American Vice-President of the time, Charles Curtis (himself part-Indian), to sit with him during the 1932 Olympic Games at Los Angeles. Later he did some extra-work in Hollywood. In 1950 an Associated Press poll voted Thorpe as the greatest athlete of the first half of the 20th century, and a year later a film of his life (*Man of Bronze*) was made, starring Burt Lancaster. Having sold the rights to his life story 20 years before, he received nothing from the film and sadly died in 1953, aged 65, as a charity case.

Although moves to get his athletic deeds reinstated began in 1943, nothing happened for years. Much of the blame for this has been laid at the door of Avery Brundage, President of the IOC from 1952 to 1972, who had been a team-mate of Thorpe's in the 1912 pentathlon and decathlon but did little to help his cause. Finally, in 1982 the IOC reinstated his name to the results and record books and the following year the gold medals were presented to his children. As a postscript, his grandson was one of the two people who jointly ran the first leg of the 1984 torch relay on American soil. The other was the granddaughter of Jesse Owens.

THE DREAM ATHLETE Though decathletes quite often produce their personal best performances in individual events during the course of a decathlon competition, they also set personal bests at other times. Thus, an interesting exercise is to calculate their total scores for a decathlon based on them reproducing their personal best in each event during one contest. Under these conditions the top man would be Dan O'Brien (USA), the 1991 World champion. His best ever marks are as follows:

First day
100m	10.23(w)	1040
LJ	8.11m(w)	1089
SP	16.69m	894
HJ	2.16m(i)	953
400m	46.53	982
		4958

Second day
110mH	13.81(w)	999
DT	52.86m	930
PV	5.25m	988
JT	62.58m	777
1500m	4:33.19	724
		4418
		9376

Britain's double Olympic champion Daley Thompson would score 9295pts, and former world record holder Jurgen Hingsen (GER) would score 9277. However, including throws recorded with the 'old' model javelin, Hingsen would increase to 9323pts and Thompson to 9315pts.

GLUTTONS FOR PUNISHMENT The decathlon and heptathlon are possibly the toughest competitions in the sport of athletics (although one would probably get a good argument from marathon runners). However, practitioners of the two events seem to delight in making

THE DREAM SCORE

Statisticians like playing around with figures, and some of the more interesting compilations that can be done are connected with the decathlon. One esoteric exercise is the mythical all-time decathlon score, based on the best marks ever achieved during decathlon competition, as follows:

Event		Athlete	Pts	
100m	10.23(w)	Dan O'Brien (USA)	1040	First day
LJ	8.11m(w)	Daley Thompson (GBR)	1089	
SP	19.17m	Edy Hubacher (SUI)	1048	
HJ	2.27m	Ralf Beilschmidt (GDR)		
		Christian Schenk (GDR)	1061	
400m	45.68	Bill Toomey (USA)	1025	

5263

Event		Athlete	Pts	
110mH	13.82*	Robert Zmelik (TCH)	998	Second day
DT	55.00m	Razvigor Jankov (BUL)	975	
PV	5.70m	Tim Bright (USA)	1132	
JT	75.84m	Enno Tjepkema (HOL)	979	
1500m	3:58.7	Robert Baker (USA)	963	

5047

10 310

(*Guy Drut (FRA) ran a hand-timed 13.5 – worth about 40 points more)

These figures take on a new significance when compared to the actual best scores ever achieved; the current world decathlon record is 8891pts by Dan O'Brien in 1992; the best ever first-day score is 4747 by O'Brien in 1991; the best ever second-day score is 4455 by Dave Johnson (USA) in 1992.

them even harder. To this end they have introduced a one-hour decathlon and a one-hour heptathlon. The last discipline in each case must be started no more than 60 minutes after the start of the first. The world best for this decathlon is 7897pts by Robert Zmelik (TCH) at Ostrava about six weeks after his Olympic triumph in 1992. He achieved the following set of marks: 10.89–7.64m–14.52m–2.08m–55.53–14.25–41.92m–4.80m–60.34m–4:55.16.

The world best for the one-hour heptathlon is held by Peggy Beer (GER) with 5915pts, set at St Moritz in July 1992. Her performances were: 13.25–1.77m–13.24m–24.64–6.16m–41.56m–2:35.28. She later placed sixth at the 1992 Olympic Games.

In 1884 a 10-discipline event called the All-Around Championship was introduced into the American championships. The events were as follows: 100y–shot–high jump–

Adding together the best performances ever achieved during a heptathlon competition, one gets a 'dream score' as follows:

100mH	.12.64	Sabine Paetz (GDR)	1179	
HJ	1.96m	Christine Stanton (AUS)	1184	First day
SP	20.94m	Eva Wilms (GER)	1263	
200m	22.30	Jackie Joyner-Kersee (USA)	1150	
			4776	
LJ	7.27m	Jackie Joyner-Kersee (USA)	1264	Second day
JT	64.64m	Tessa Sanderson (GBR)	1145	
800m	2:01.84	Nadine Debois (FRA)	1087	
			3496	
			8272	

880y walk–hammer–pole vault–120y hurdles–56lb weight throw–long jump–mile, all to be contested in one day. The 1904 Olympic 'decathlon' consisted of the same ten events held on the same day.

A PERFECT WOMAN, NOBLY PLANNED (*William Wordsworth*) The equivalent event to the decathlon for women is the heptathlon, and one can play the same statistical games with this. The double Olympic heptathlon champion Jackie Joyner-Kersee (USA) is even further ahead of the opposition in terms of best-ever performances than she is under competition conditions. Her current world record is 7291pts, set at Seoul in September 1988. Her best ever marks give the following scores:

First day

100mH	12.61	1184
HJ	1.93m	1145
SP	16.84m	985
200m	22.30	1150
		4464

Second day

LJ	7.45m	1327
JT	50.12m	862
800m	2:08.51	987
		3176
		7640

DOUBLE, DOUBLE, TOIL AND TROUBLE

The zenith of athletic masochism was reached at Punkalaidun, Finland on 12–13 September 1992, when world bests were achieved in the **Double-Decathlon** and **Double-Heptathlon**. The events in the men's contest were the following: (First day) 100m–long jump–200m hurdles–shot–5000m–800m–high jump–400m–hammer–3000m steeplechase; (second day) 110m hurdles–discus–200m–pole vault–3000m–400m hurdles–javelin–1500m–triple jump–10 000m. Indrek Kaseorg of Estonia beat his previous record with a total of 14 274 points.

In the women's contest the events ran as follows: (First day) 100m hurdles–high jump–1500m–400m hurdles–shot–200m; (second day) 100m–long jump–400m–javelin–800m–discus–3000m. Irina Stasenko of Russia improved her record to 10 824 points. Lest anyone should think that the athletes concerned were only minor ones, a look at the performances achieved, taking into account the severity of this gruelling test, should allay that thought.

INDREK KASEORG

(First day)

100m	11.75
LJ	7.00m
200mH	25.01
SP	12.13m
5000m	17:36.07
800m	2:04.84
HJ	1.99m
400m	50.72
HT	32.26m
3000mSt	10:50.14

(Second day)

110mH	15.11
DT	37.04m
200m	23.20
PV	4.30m
3000m	10:18.50
400mH	54.00
JT	57.78m
1500m	4:47.36
TJ	14.05m
10 000m	45:35.95

IRINA STASENKO

(First day)

100mH	14.95
HJ	1.57m
1500m	4:44.41
400mH	61.82
SP	12.71m
200m	25.58

(Second day)

100m	12.86
LJ	5.66m
400m	59.09
JT	37.52m
800m	2:17.88
200mH	28.98
DT	30.32m
3000m	10:46.93

The best regular decathlon score achieved by Kaseorg is 7826pts in 1992, while the best heptathlon score by Stasenko is 5607 in 1990, but it seems likely that their concentration on the 'double' event has prevented them scoring much higher in the standard contests.

WALK ON, WALK ON, WITH HOPE IN YOUR HEART

ANONYMOUS

'Competing at race-walking is the closest a man can come to experiencing the pangs of childbirth'

ERNESTO CANTO (1984 Olympic 20km walk champion from Mexico)

'If you want to be the best then you can hardly complain that it was too hot, too cold, too hard, or too easy; you have to be ready for all conditions'

RON LAIRD (US Olympic walker – on how devoted he was in his youth to sport)

'Let me put it this way. I had my first date at the age of 22'

> **WILLIAM SHAKESPEARE**
> (*Rosalind in* As You Like It)
>
> *'TIME TRAVELS IN DIVERS PACES WITH DIVERS PERSONS. I'LL TELL YOU WHO TIME AMBLES WITHAL, WHO TIME TROTS WITHAL, WHO TIME GALLOPS WITHAL, AND WHO HE STANDS STILL WITHAL'*

WILL YOU WALK A LITTLE FASTER, SAID A WHITING TO A SNAIL (*Lewis Carroll*) The 1948 Olympic 10km track walk set the seal on future track walks in major championships. Firstly, there were quite outrageous chauvinistic decisions made by some of the judges (not least by the Swedes against the British). Secondly, even to the uninitiated it was obvious that many of the competitors were breaking the rules on 'lifting' to a remarkable degree. The final straw came in the last 100 metres of the final, when the chief judge Georgio Oberweger of Italy (a former discus medallist and a very fit man) was unable to catch the second- and third-placed Fritz Schwab of Switzerland and Bruno Junk of the Soviet Union, to disqualify them – because they were running faster than he was!

CREEPS IN THIS PETTY PACE FROM DAY TO DAY (*Macbeth*) The famous Scottish pedestrian, Capt. Barclay Allardice, made a wager to walk 1000 miles in 1000 consecutive hours at Newmarket in 1809, in which he had to cover a mile within each hour. His winnings amounted to £16 000 (which at today's rates would be in the region of £180 000).

STILL ACHIEVING, STILL PURSUING (*Henry Wadsworth Longfellow*) British walker Bob Dobson has featured in the top 12 national rankings in the 50km walk for an unprecedented 24 years from 1969 to 1992. He has clocked a sub-5 hour time for the distance on 100 occasions (to the end of the 1992 season). He won five national titles and held the British record for the 50km walk from 1974 to 1980.

A WALK ON THE WILD SIDE

One of the greatest Olympians, and certainly one of the greatest walkers, was Vladimir Golubnichiy of the Soviet Union. Competing in the same event, the 20km walk, in five celebrations from 1960 to 1976, he placed successively 1st, 3rd, 1st, 2nd and 7th (as a 40-year-old), an unmatched record in a single event. Additionally he gained gold, silver and bronze medals in the European championships.

WHAT THE COACH SAID

ARTHUR LYDIARD (famous New Zealand coach)

'You must realise that some people are born with a Rolls-Royce engine, while others only get a Volkswagen one'

PERCY CERUTTY (famed Australian coach and philosopher)

'Nothing worthwhile is easily achieved, and nothing easily achieved is worthwhile. That is why talent in itself is an insufficient key to success'

PAUL LABUSCHAGNE (coach of South African star Elana Meyer, in 1991)

'She's a strange person, she's completely relaxed under pressure. International competition is not about doing a certain number of laps around the track. It's putting up with flight delays and training in strange places, and Elana can handle all those disruptions'

TOMMY BOYLE (coach to Yvonne Murray and Tom McKean)

'For the coach, planning schedules and standing on the track with the watch is the easy bit. Getting the mental preparation right is the big challenge'

ANONYMOUS COACH

'Look at him. He has a perfect record. He don't smoke, he don't drink, he don't chase women, and he don't win'

CLYDE HART (Michael Johnson's coach – on why his athlete declined the offer to run in a preliminary heat of the 1991 world championships 4 × 400m relay)

'That's an insult. That's like asking Michelangelo to paint the outside of the Vatican, but getting Joe Blow to paint the ceiling'

TOM McNAB (British athletics coach and author)

'I am not, nor have I ever claimed to be, Mother Theresa, selflessly pursuing athletics coaching for the good of the young, and I would give short shrift to anyone who claimed that as his primary motive. I coach because I find it fun, and when it ceases to be fun I will stop doing it'

BRIAN SCOBIE (British coach living in the USA, in 1992)

'It is important for high demands to be placed upon the elite athlete in training, but it is also important that they are met. Elite athletes are as susceptible to doubts and fears as ordinary mortals. . . . Success at elite level is so significantly determined by psychological factors that it is difficult to over-emphasise this aspect of the coach-athlete relationship'

ARTHUR LYDIARD (famous New Zealand coach)

'I use 200m to determine basic speed, because anything less can be influenced by the quickness of the start, and anything longer brings in stamina'

SAY WHAT YOU MEAN . . .

'PUSH IT!'
(You've got no guts)

'WHAT HE NEEDS ISN'T A COACH, BUT A PSYCHIATRIST'
(What the hell is he doing?)

'HE'S GOT TO DIG DEEPER'
(He's had it)

'SHE'S LAYING OFF THE PACE'
(She's miles behind)

'NOT MUCH FURTHER'
(About 4½ miles of rough country)

'POWERING DOWN THE BACK STRAIGHT'
(Athletes never seem to power at other places on the track)

'HE'S OBVIOUSLY BEEN DOING A LOT OF WEIGHT TRAINING'
(He's muscle-bound)

'THE STRIDE PATTERN'S ALL WRONG' *(The twit)*

'LOST IT ALL AT THE END'
(Chickened-out)

'OFF THE BEND THEY'RE NECK AND NECK'
(Great television)

'THEY'RE SURGING'
(They've stopped jogging and are making an honest race of it)

'HE'S CHECKING HIS TAKE-OFF MARK'
(He messed up the last jump)

'HE'S CALLING IT A DAY'
(He's got his bonus for the record so why do more)

'THERE ARE 4 KENYANS IN THE STEEPLECHASE'
(Everyone else might as well go home)

'IT'S A TESTING COURSE'
(It has some 1-in-7 hills)

DINK TEMPLETON (Stanford University coach to quarter-miler Ben Eastman in March 1932)

'Go right out from the gun and run just as fast as you can. Run easily, without effort, but run like hell'

(Eastman broke the world record for 440y by a full second with 46.4sec after passing 220y in 21.3sec)

TOMMY BOYLE (coach to Tom McKean, British 800m runner, at start of 1992)

'Well, Tom, you've now made every mistake there is to make in the book. There is no other error even you can make. In fact, you've done the lot, so this must be your year'

FRANK DICK (Britain's National Director of Coaching)

'Money is better managed in British athletics than it is in any sport that I've come across'

RON PICKERING (coach and broadcaster)

'Sport was born of philosophers and teachers and has survived 33 centuries because it is based on the ethics of fair play. Athletics is special to me because it caters for the young and the old, the fat and the thin, the best and the beginner. Sport is the most precious commodity we have to hand on to the next generation'

ARTHUR LYDIARD (famed New Zealand coach)

'For me, world-class runners always have been just a part of the cake. The

greatest challenge for a coach is to help an ordinary runner – one with no talent at all – to become a good one. To make a 2:30-marathoner out of a 2:50-man, that is really something'

ANONYMOUS COACH (talking of a former athlete)

'I told him, "Son, I can't understand what it is with you. Is it ignorance or apathy?" He said, "Coach, I don't know and what is more I don't care."'

TOM MESCHERY (basketball coach, in the 1970s)

'There was a time, and it was not so long ago, when things such as honour and loyalty were virtues in sport and

not objects of ridicule. There was a time when athletes drew pleasure and satisfaction from the essence of competition not just from their paychecks'

COACH/ATHLETE DISCUSSION

A: *'I'm dynamite in the finishing straight'*

C: *'Yes, you always blow up'*

JOHNNY SAIN (baseball coach – reaction to complaints about hard training)

'The world doesn't want to hear about labour pains. It only wants to see the baby'

LIFE AFTER SPORT

PEACE IN OUR TIME One of the more remarkable lives of the 20th century was surely that of the aforementioned Philip Baker. Born into a Quaker family in London, he first went to college in Pennsylvania and then on to King's College, Cambridge. While there, he blossomed into a fine middle-distance runner, making the British team and placing sixth in the 1912 Olympic 1500m. During World War I he refused to carry arms, as a confirmed pacifist, but joined an ambulance unit and was decorated for distinguished conduct. In 1919 he was in the British contingent to the Peace Conference and later worked for the League of Nations. In 1920 he was a member of the Olympic team again, and this time gained the 1500m silver medal behind his team-mate Albert Hill. Adding his wife's maiden name to his own, he became a Labour MP as Philip Noel-Baker and at one time was Secretary of State for Air. Throughout he campaigned for peace, and wrote a well received book *The Arms Race: A Programme for Disarmament*, published in 1958. The following year he was awarded the Nobel Peace Prize. He became a Peer and died in 1982, just short of his 93rd birthday.

I HAVE A SONG TO SING, O Among singers with athletic backgrounds are pop star Johnny Mathis, a 1.96m high jumper at college; opera star Anne Pashley, British bronze medallist in the 1954 European 100m; Scottish folk singer Moira Kerr, a former international shot putter; and the late Paul Robeson, who was an excellent college high jumper.

FAME IS THE SPUR A number of athletes have made excellent careers for themselves in the civil service or government of their respective countries.

Perhaps the greatest heights were reached by Arthur Porritt GCMG, GCVO, CBE, winner of the bronze medal in the 1924 Olympic 100m. He was a surgeon to the Queen, Governor-General of New Zealand from 1967 to 1972, and was created a Baron in 1973.

Dr Arthur Wint, MBE, won the 1948 Olympic 400m title for Jamaica while studying in Britain after RAF service during the war. Later he was appointed Jamaican High Commissioner in London (1974) and Ambassador to Sweden (1975).

Major-General Robert Kotei was Defence Minister of Ghana until he was shot in June 1979. In Britain as a cadet at Sandhurst, he had been bronze medallist in the 1958 Commonwealth Games high jump and won the 1960 AAA title. Mahamat Idriss was the first high jumper from Africa to clear 2.13m (*7ft*) and at the unusually young age of 21 he became Minister of Youth and Sport in Chad.

In 1981 Habib Thiam became Prime Minister of Senegal. While studying in France he had won their 200m title on two occasions. The former Prime Minister of Jamaica, Michael Manley, had been national junior 100y record holder in 1911. In December 1991, Trinidad's Wendell Mottley, who won the 400m silver medal in the 1964 Olympics, was elected to his country's Parliament and made Minister of Finance (he was a graduate of Yale and Cambridge universities).

Three heads of state had impressive athletic credentials in their youth. Dr Urho Kekkonen, President of Finland 1956–81, was the Finnish high jump champion in 1924. Paul Kruger, President of the Boer Republic (1883–1902) is said to have long-jumped a then world best of 7.01m (*23ft 0in*) in 1845. The inaugural President of the United States, George Washington, is similarly reputed to have long-jumped about 6.78m (*22ft 3in*).

Prior to his marital and weight 'problems', King Henry VIII was known as an excellent athlete, particularly good at long jumping, while Henry V also had a reputation as a runner of ability.

In the United States, Dave Bolen, fourth in the 1948 Olympic 400m, was appointed Ambassador to Botswana, Lesotho and Swaziland in

1974. Double Olympic decathlon champion (1948–52) Bob Mathias was elected to the Congress in 1966, while 1936 Olympic relay gold medallist Ralph Metcalfe was elected to the House of Representatives in 1970.

In Great Britain the recent election of two-time Olympic 1500m champion Sebastian Coe to the House of Commons drew attention to other athletes who made their mark in the 'Mother of Parliaments'. The first Olympic champion to enter the House was 1928 400m hurdles winner Lord Burghley. A contemporary of his was Philip Noel-Baker (see page opposite). Between 1970 and 1974 Chris Chataway, former world

Ladies and gentlemen, the President of the United States!

5000m record holder, was Minister of Posts & Telecommunications and then Minister for Industrial Development. A 1952 Olympian Terence Higgins KBE, 400m and relay, is a former Minister of State at the Treasury and is the long-time MP for Worthing. The Liberal Democrats defence spokesman Menzies Campbell was a member of the 1964 Olympic sprint team and held the British 100m record for a time.

Elsewhere, former women's sprint world record holder Chi Cheng became a deputy in the Taiwan parliament in 1981, and Ruth Fuchs, twice Olympic javelin champion (1972–76), and her teammate Gunhild Hoffmeister, the 1974 European 1500m champion, were members of the GDR parliament. In 1992 Fuchs was elected to the Bundestag, the united German Parliament.

NONE BUT THE BRAVE Many athletes have gained their country's highest decorations for bravery during war, but none have matched the honours of Captain Noel Godfrey Chavasse of the Royal Army Medical Corps in World War I. In the 1908 Olympics both he and his twin, Christopher, then students at Oxford University, ran for Britain in the 400m. In the War he was awarded the MC, the VC and then posthumously, a bar to the VC.

A FOREIGN FIELD A marker was erected in China in 1991 near the site of the Japanese internment camp at Weifang, in memory of Britain's Eric Liddell, the 1924 Olympic 400m champion. Liddell,

one of the heroes of the film *Chariots of Fire*, became a missionary, was interned by the Japanese and died there in 1945.

HOW ARE THE MIGHTY FALLEN Ronald Reagan, then President of the United States, speaking at a fund-raising dinner for the US Olympic Committee in 1983, recalled that he once had aspirations of being an Olympic athlete. However, they were dashed when his high school 4 × 220y relay team, of which he was a valued member, lost in the Illinois State Championships to another school whose team included an athlete named Ralph Metcalfe.

THE SHOWBIZ CONNECTION A number of top-class athletes have made careers for themselves in the world of entertainment, in particular in the movies. One of the first, and probably one of the most successful, was Herman Brix, the 1928 Olympic shot silver medallist. As Bruce Bennett he made his name as Tarzan in *The New Adventures of Tarzan* (1935) but later became a good dramatic actor in many films. The 1936 Olympic decathlon champion Glenn Morris also played Tarzan in *Tarzan's Revenge*, in which his co-star was Olympic swimming champion Eleanor Holm.

INDEX